The Good Divorce

Guide

The Good Divorce Guide

*Facing reality when
your world is upside-down*

Teresa J. Payne
&
Vanessa Gardiner

First edition published 2017
© Teresa J. Payne

Published by
www.elitepublishingacademy.com

Printed and bound in Great Britain by
www.n2printondemand.co.uk

A catalogue record for this book
is available from The British Library
ISBN 978-1-910090-28-2

Disclaimer and Invitation

We hope you find the information contained in this book helpful. Please remember every divorce is different and you should make sure you obtain the best settlement possible for you in your circumstances. We advise you to actually speak to a family solicitor personally, because they'll be able to help with your individual situation and provide bespoke advice for you.

If you're ready to talk to a solicitor, we'd like to invite you to a free, face-to-face meeting (valued at £200) with one of our expert family lawyers. You can come to any of our offices and be sure to find a solicitor who will understand your individual needs and who will look after your best interests.

Simply call 0800 015 2843.

Or email tgdg@parfittcresswell.com and book a time to come and tell us about your relationship.

Acknowledgements

Although there are just two names on the cover, it's certainly not solely our book. We wouldn't have been able to write it without the expert contributions (and moral support) of everyone on the Family Law Team at Parfitt Cresswell.

We'd like to thank Zanariah Webster, Javita Malhotra, Sharon Micuta, and Elizabeth Jones for their contributions — and everyone on the Family Law Team who works so hard to help our clients move onto the next stage of their lives with hope and happiness.

And, of course, we'd like to thank our wonderful clients who've allowed us to share their experiences with you. They have moved onto exciting futures, and they hope their experiences will help you do the same.

Contents

INTRODUCTION: You're Not Alone   1

CHAPTER 1: Divorce Demystified   7

CHAPTER 2: You Have Options: Alternative Dispute Resolution   25

CHAPTER 3: Keeping Costs Under Control   55

CHAPTER 4: Making Sense of Finances   73

CHAPTER 5: Attention! Business Owners   97

CHAPTER 6: Think of the Children   109

CHAPTER 7: How to Cope with an Abusive Partner   131

CHAPTER 8: Getting Married   147

NEXT STEPS   153

Jargon Explained   161

About the Author   169

Introduction: You're Not Alone

Everything You Need to Know to Survive Divorce — and Come Out Positive

The end of a relationship can feel like the end of the world — and in some ways, it is. If you're facing divorce, an entire chapter of your life is coming to an end. The person you thought you'd be spending the rest of your life with will no longer be your partner.

Everything will be different, everything seems to happen at once — and if you're lying awake at night worrying, please know you're not the only one.

You probably have dozens of questions spinning around your head. Questions like:

"What does my future hold? Will I be happy again? What did I do wrong? What could I have done instead? Am I making the right decision? What if I can't cope on my own? How do I protect my children and my family? Where do I even start, and who can I trust to look out for my interests?"

All those questions are perfectly natural and we want you to know you're not alone.

Because, sadly, more than 50% of marriages in the UK eventually fall apart. It can be the most traumatic time in your life as things finally come to a head after months — and in some cases, years — deciding whether or not to stay together.

When you've finally made the decision to move on alone, you expect it to come as a relief... but instead, there are a thousand-and-one things to worry about.

We'd love to be able to tell you divorce can be a breeze, but the truth is — there's no easy way out.

Getting divorced is upsetting even under the best of circumstances, but you don't have to go through it alone. Lean on your friends and family for emotional support — and let us help you take care of the practical challenges.

That's what this book is all about. We want to reassure you you're not alone, divorce doesn't have to be as complicated and traumatic and confrontational as you may fear, and you *can* come out of it stronger and happier.

We also want to lay to rest any myths you may have heard or believed about divorce. Unlike in the bad old days, you can arrange the end of your marriage with very little fuss and cost.

"Do I really need a solicitor?"

It's true divorce is much simpler and fairer than it used to be, but there are still complex procedures to follow and documents to file. This can be a minefield for the inexperienced and unwary — particularly when emotions are running high and rationality has a tendency to fly out of the window.

A good solicitor will help you navigate the whole process, will give you invaluable advice and support, and will prevent you from making any errors that will slow things down or harm your own interests.

In short, a good solicitor will help you get the best outcome for everyone, with as little fuss, cost, and stress as possible.

Many people fear solicitors will take advantage of people at their most vulnerable time — but a good solicitor would never do that. Contrary to popular belief, we don't have hearts of stone, and many of us have been through exactly what you're going through now.

Choose your solicitor carefully, and they'll be your rock, have your back, and encourage you to work towards the fairest outcome for *everyone*: you, your spouse, your children, and your family.

Incidentally, you'll often hear the terms "solicitor", "divorce lawyer", "family lawyer", and "family law solicitor" — and they can all mean the same thing. "Lawyer" is a generic term which describes anyone who is licensed to practise law. When someone uses any of these words, they usually mean a solicitor or legal executive who specialises in family and divorce law.

Barristers are also divorce lawyers, but you'll usually see a solicitor at first, and you may never need to see a barrister. Barristers can be involved for a number of reasons, for example if the case is complex and there are court proceedings. If this is your situation, your solicitor and barrister will work as a team to make sure you have the very best representation of your case to the judge.

Or, it may be more cost-effective to instruct a barrister to go to a court hearing — especially if the court is some distance from where your solicitor is based. Barristers often wear a wig and gown in court, but this tends to be rare in family courts. They may also work at higher levels of court than solicitors.

A barrister's main role is as an advocate in legal hearings — they stand in court and plead their client's case in front of a judge.

"Where do I start?"

This book gives you all the information you need to start the divorce process and choose the right solicitor for you. It walks you through common myths and misconceptions — and shows you what's really involved.

You'll discover how to deal with the practicalities of finances, funding, children, businesses, and families — and how to negotiate with your spouse calmly and rationally so everyone gets the best possible outcome.

In Chapter 1, you'll discover exactly what divorce is and what it involves — and how to navigate the process with as little fuss, stress, and cost as possible.

In Chapter 2, we'll lay out all your options for navigating your divorce with your spouse and for working with solicitors on both sides.

Chapter 3 is all about funding: how to pay for your divorce, even if you're struggling.

In Chapter 4, we'll look at your finances as a couple and what you need to consider. You'll discover how to protect your assets; how to make arrangements for pensions, maintenance, mortgages, and wills; and what to consider if you ever get married again.

Chapter 5 covers business ownership and helps you think through everything you need to consider if you want to protect your business — or divide it fairly.

In Chapter 6, you'll discover how children are affected by divorce and how to ensure you get the best outcome for them.

Chapter 7 is all about domestic violence under the law — and what you need to know.

And Chapter 8 is all about what happens next. How to move forwards and even how to stay friends with your ex-spouse.

Who is this book for?

We've written this book for people who are in the midst of a relationship breakdown, or who are already starting the divorce process. It's for anyone who's uncertain, confused, or frightened about what the future holds and how to navigate divorce.

It's for people who want the best outcome and future for everyone: for their ex-spouse, their children, their families, and their friends — because divorce doesn't have to become a war zone and it doesn't have to become a fight for supremacy. If you want to make a new start, rather than gear up for a big fight, this book will help you do just that.

If you read this book carefully, and refer back to it whenever you need to, you'll have a much better idea of what to expect. Over the years, we've found it's not specific events that people fear; it's the unknown.

That's why we wrote this book: to demystify divorce and to break down any fears you may have. To take you from a frightening, uncertain present to a well-informed, well-prepared future. We're here to advise you and help you work through your divorce, *not* tell you what to do. This is all about finding what's best for you, your spouse, and your family — and making it happen.

We want you to be able to stop dwelling on the past and start looking forward to and planning for a happy future. It is possible — that we promise you.

Teresa J Payne & Vanessa Gardiner
Parfitt Cresswell

Chapter 1

Divorce Demystified

Truths and Myths

Whatever myths exist about getting a divorce must be laid to rest. It's no longer the preserve of old men in wigs and judgemental court cases: the whole procedure has been modernised, meaning you can arrange the end of your marriage with very little fuss and cost.

The reality is, the amount of paperwork is steadily decreasing and the forms themselves are getting simpler. Divorce is no longer about dragging people through the courts; it's all about form-filling and including only what's necessary to finalise the divorce.

The bad old days of hearing evidence in every case and considering childcare arrangements in court have long since passed — so don't let the process itself frighten you off.

The most difficult part of any divorce is always emotional — and, of course, the real practicalities of ending a relationship and splitting a shared life into two separate ones.

But no matter how painful the end of a relationship is, it should never be necessary to make things more difficult.

That's why you can now resolve any problems arising from your marriage *outside* the courts, through negotiation directly with your ex-partner or through your solicitor, mediation, arbitration, collaborative law, and round table negotiations. This is called Alternative Dispute Resolution (ADR) — and your solicitor will help you find the most suitable method.

Although things are much simpler now, your solicitor is always your best port of call to find out where you stand on divorce, separation, and financial issues — including any questions or concerns you may have about domestic violence or arrangements for children.

The law is simpler, to be sure; but it's still a minefield for the inexperienced and unfamiliar. As your case moves forward, you may need to seek further advice and support. A good solicitor will be invaluable here, helping you lodge applications, attending hearings on your behalf, or drafting documents to help with a hearing.

Chapter 1 is all about the divorce process itself: we're going to explain exactly what's involved, then go through and shoot down some of the most common myths and misconceptions.

Staying in Control of Your Emotions

First, though, we want to say a few words about the human side of divorce. The legal side of divorce can seem like a cold process — let's not forget humans are messy, emotional creatures...

When a relationship ends, there's always one person who's reached the decision to separate before the other. In a way, they'll have the emotional advantage because they'll have had time to build up to that decision — which may have come as a shock to their partner.

Keep this in mind when you start talking about negotiations and settlements — because the person who makes the decision to leave will already be thinking about the future... while their partner has been left behind. The person at the emotional disadvantage may find it very difficult to settle at first, because their emotions will be very raw.

A good family lawyer will have many years of experience dealing with divorce and separation. He or she will understand the importance of being open, compassionate, and understanding, especially at the start of the process.

Before your solicitor puts forward any settlement proposal for you, they should do everything they can to make sure you can make a rational decision about whether or not to go ahead with it.

This is where the skill of an experienced family solicitor really comes into play — it's as much about being able to provide the emotional support that keeps your divorce out of the courts as it is about providing expert legal advice.

When we work with clients, we often refer them to a counsellor or mentor to help them cope and work through their emotions. Ultimately, of course, how you proceed is up to you — but it's best for everyone involved if you do whatever you need to do to make sure you're prepared for what's to come.

If you or your spouse rush in while emotions are still high, that's when mistakes are made and things get very painful. Don't be afraid to take a little time out for yourself to come to terms with what's happening before coming back to your solicitor if you feel you need to — you'll find the process much easier if you do.

What Is Divorce?

A marriage is a legally binding relationship — so if a couple no longer wants to be part of that relationship, they'll need to consider getting divorced to break the legal ties to their spouse.

Not every married couple that splits up gets divorced right away; some simply separate instead.

If you're not sure what to do, talk to a family law solicitor who'll be able to talk you through the legal and practical implications of divorce, compared to separation.

Whether you divorce or separate, you'll still need to deal with the financial and other aspects of ending a relationship — all of which this book will help you with.

If you've been married for less than a year, you can't legally apply for a divorce — but you do have other options, which we'll explain later in this chapter.

What Do You Need to get Divorced?

There's only one ground for divorce: the marriage has irretrievably broken down. That sounds simple enough — but you have to prove it with one of five facts:

- Unreasonable behaviour
- Adultery
- Two years' desertion
- Two years' separation with spouse's consent
- Five years' separation

The most common reason given for divorce is "unreasonable behaviour" which can cause real problems because it feels like assigning blame — which is not a good start if you want to keep things amicable.

Unfortunately, though, if you don't want to wait years for a divorce, it's the only option. So it's really important to talk things through with your spouse and make it clear that "unreasonable behaviour" is simply a means to an end.

The ideal solution would be to put a "no fault" system in place so couples can divorce without any suggestion of blame. There's a lot of debate in the legal world over this issue and a Bill was presented to the Government to provide for such a system — but at the time of writing, no such plans are on the cards.

Once you've got your reason sorted out, you'll need some other things, too.

- **Your original marriage certificate** (or a certified copy if the original was lost or destroyed). If you got married abroad, you can still get divorced as long as you fulfilled the criteria for marriage in that country. Ask your solicitor to check the marriage certificate — and you'll need an official translation if it's not in English.

- **Your spouse's address.** If you have no idea where your spouse is living, you may still be able to go ahead with a divorce — but you'll need to talk to your solicitor about what you'll need to do to try and find your spouse's address. Be aware that it could delay things and cost more money.

- **Correct forms and fees.** Your solicitor can deal with the divorce petition for you. You can complete the form yourself — but we'd advise getting a solicitor to check it over, because it's an important legal document. If you make a mistake, it could cost you dearly in terms of the divorce itself and the fees. You'll also need the correct fees to pay the court and your solicitor. You can find the current court fee for issuing a divorce petition at www.gov.uk/court-fees-what-they-are.

Many solicitors, including our own firm, provide free initial consultations so you can talk over the likely cost before making any commitments.

The Divorce Process

The first step is the Divorce Petition. The petitioner is the person who issues the paperwork at court and the respondent is the spouse who receives the papers.

The court needs evidence that the respondent knows about the divorce proceedings, so when the respondent receives the paperwork, they must acknowledge it by filling in the Acknowledgement of Service form, and returning it to the court.

The court tells the petitioner (or their solicitor) and sends a copy of the Acknowledgement of Service form so they can apply for the next stage.

If the respondent doesn't return the paperwork to court, you'll need to consider your options to move forwards. You might be able to prove the respondent has received the papers in another way — alternatively, you can instruct a court bailiff or a process server to serve the papers personally. This increases costs, so you'll want to avoid this if you can. Your solicitor will be able to help you if you run into problems here.

It's fairly common for people to fail to return the Acknowledgement of Service form for a variety of reasons — after all, emotions are running high, and some people may not want to face reality. But it's not usually a serious problem.

It is quite rare, however, for someone to refuse to accept reality completely and object to the divorce petition being issued. In legal jargon, this is called "defending the petition". There are two main reasons for doing so: firstly, the respondent may deny the marriage has irretrievably broken down or disagree on the grounds for divorce.

Secondly, the respondent may decide to cross petition — which means they admit the marriage has broken down, but *they* want to be the one petitioning for divorce instead.

The Decree Nisi

When it's clear the respondent knows about the divorce process and agrees to it (or at least isn't planning to object), the petitioner can apply for a decree nisi.

"Decree nisi" comes from the Latin words meaning "a rule unless". It's a court order that has no force unless a particular condition is met. In the case of divorce, it says the marriage can be dissolved as long as nobody brings forward evidence to the contrary within the next six weeks.

At this point, the judge considers the divorce petition and decides whether or not the petitioner has given sufficient reasons for the marriage breaking down. Then the judge will set a date for pronouncing the decree nisi. The court deals with this, but you don't have to actually attend court unless you're disputing costs.

When the decree nisi is pronounced, the petitioner (or their solicitor) will receive the Decree Nisi Certificate.

The Decree Absolute

Six weeks and one day after the decree nisi has been pronounced, the petitioner can apply for the decree absolute — the document confirming the marriage has been dissolved. It's the court's final order officially ending a marriage.

If the petitioner fails to apply for the decree absolute, the respondent can do so 18 weeks and one day from the decree nisi. There are a few reasons why you might want to delay applying for the decree absolute — for example if there are still financial matters to resolve. So do take advice from your solicitor before applying.

You can stop divorce proceedings at any time, right up until the decree absolute is issued.

Is There an Alternative to Divorce?

There is — usually if you've been married for less than a year or you object to divorce on religious grounds. You can apply for a decree of judicial separation instead.

This is a court order and is similar to a divorce. You'd remain legally married — but your normal marital obligations cease and you don't have to go on living together. Normally, people who obtain a decree of judicial separation don't necessarily want to divorce — perhaps for religious or moral reasons — but want to live apart from their spouse with enough formality to allow them to each live their own lives.

You can get a decree of judicial separation for any of the grounds that would justify a divorce — but you *don't* have to prove the marriage has irretrievably broken down.

It has three main effects:

1. You're no longer obliged to live together.
2. The court can divide all property and assets just as if you were getting divorced.
3. It will have the same effects as divorce on any will.

Unless you've been married for less than a year, or both partners are opposed to divorce for religious reasons, it's hard to see how it could be in anyone's interest to agree to a decree of judicial separation rather than divorce.

In fact, it could store up many problems for the future, particularly if one or both people meet someone else and want to remarry. And if you do decide to get divorced in future, you'll need to go through the whole divorce procedure from the start, paying all the costs to do so.

We would strongly advise you to get legal advice before agreeing to a decree of judicial separation.

Another alternative is a Separation Agreement, in which you'll agree to live apart. You should also include clauses dealing with financial arrangements, including division of assets and payment of maintenance.

A separation agreement is just like any other contract, so rules apply. This means it might not be as easy to enforce financial arrangements as an order you'd obtain in a divorce. However, it can offer a degree of flexibility that can be helpful. Remember, you can't achieve the same finality with a separation agreement — so you'll want to consider this before making any decisions. Whether you're divorcing or separating, you should always review your will and carefully consider your financial situation to ensure everyone is left in the best situation.

Common Divorce Myths

There's something about emotional upheaval that makes rumours fly around — so there's a variety of myths and misconceptions about marriage and divorce law.

Many people are shocked to discover the outcome they expect isn't possible. So let's look at the most common myths...

"I've got a common-law marriage…"

Contrary to popular belief, there's no such thing as a "common-law marriage" — in the UK at least. Some people mistakenly believe if you and your partner have been living together for long enough, you'll be recognised as married in the eyes of the law — whether or not that's actually the case. This isn't true.

No matter how long you've lived together, the courts won't recognise you as a married couple unless you're actually legally married, so if you separate, you'll need to use the civil courts, not the legal ones.

"My partner was unfaithful and abusive, so I'm entitled to everything!"

Regardless of how upsetting and damaging adultery and domestic abuse may be, they have no effect on the financial assessment during a divorce case.

"Mothers are always granted custody of the children."

Although it's certainly common that the mother has the children living with her, it's not a hard and fast rule.

The Children's Act 1989 states clearly that a child's welfare is the court's paramount consideration. Courts will always encourage you and your partner to make your own arrangements without getting them involved.

If you really can't work it out together, the court decides based on what's best for the children. For example, if there was evidence the mother was incapable of looking after the children alone, the court would ask for reports to confirm it. Or if the mother worked full-time while the father stayed at home to look after the children, the court may decide it's in the children's best interests to stay with their dad.

"Grandparents have no visitation rights."
Grandparents do not have automatic rights to have contact with the grandchildren under the law in England and Wales. However, if one parent is preventing grandparents from visiting, grandparents can apply to the court to have contact with their grandchildren.

If there are existing court proceedings relating to the children, grandparents can ask the court to make them a party to the case — which means they can be represented at court.

Otherwise, grandparents must ask permission of the court to apply for contact. If permission is granted, the court will decide based on the children's long-term wellbeing. Unless there are very good reasons to prevent grandparents from seeing their grandchildren, the courts are likely to order parents to allow contact with the children.

"Divorce is always expensive."
We've seen exaggerated estimates in the tabloid newspapers of typical divorces costing £100,000. This is

not true — and unless you live in a world of expensive London lawyers, and extremely complicated proceedings, and perhaps the Court of Appeal, your fees won't be anything like this.

In a normal case in a provincial county court, it's nowhere near that bad. Divorce isn't cheap… but it's not extortionate. Costs will rise if you're unfortunate enough not to reach a settlement early in negotiations, and will rise further if you go to a final hearing.

"I want a quickie divorce"

There's no such thing. In America, you could get a "quickie divorce" by going south of the border to Mexico, which is probably where the idea came from. But all divorces in England and Wales take about the same amount of time, whatever the grounds. If you use adultery or unreasonable behaviour as your reason, you can start the divorce immediately and wrap everything up within a few months. With desertion or separation, it's a minimum of two years, possibly longer.

"Mediation is all about saving the marriage"

Mediation is not the same as marriage guidance counselling, and the purpose isn't to save your marriage. Mediation is all about finding a solution to your dispute. It helps you resolve your differences with as little strife as possible — and it helps you avoid damaging your relationship further, which is particularly important if you have children.

Couples sometimes do reconcile during mediation, but it's rare, and it's not the primary purpose.

"I want a divorce on the grounds of irreconcilable differences."

Unfortunately, this isn't an option in England and Wales. To get a divorce, you must show your marriage has irretrievably broken down as a result of either adultery, unreasonable behaviour, two years' desertion, two years' separation (with your spouse's consent), or five years' separation.

"You must have a solicitor to get divorced."

You can represent yourself if you want to; you don't have to get a solicitor. However, although divorce is much simpler than it used to be, it's very easy to come unstuck if you're not experienced in family law. You risk losing out on a fair or reasonable financial settlement, and the financial consent order can be a very complicated legal document.

We strongly recommend you appoint a solicitor, if for no other reason than to check everything over.

Remember, too, that a good family solicitor will also take away a lot of extra stress and worry at a time when you'll already be under a lot of strain.

"Solicitors always go to court — I don't want that"

Court is only necessary if you can't reach an agreement, or if one partner is not willing to co-operate. Only a small number of cases lead to court applications — and only a tiny number of those cases go all the way to trial. Courts encourage people to negotiate — and so do good, conscientious solicitors.

Contrary to popular belief, the last thing solicitors want is a vicious fight. Many family lawyers are members of Resolution — our firm included — and we abide by its Code of Practice, which always encourages a non-confrontational approach.

Summary

- Divorce is the final dissolution of a legal marriage — to get started, you'll need to decide on the reason for the "irretrievable breakdown" of your marriage; you'll need your original marriage certificate, your spouse's address, and the correct forms and fees.

- The divorce petitioner applies for a decree nisi when the respondent acknowledges the divorce proceedings.

- The decree absolute is issued six weeks and one day after the decree nisi is pronounced — as long as no objections are raised or matters are outstanding.

In Chapter 2, we'll look at your options for working through your divorce proceedings, including: mediation, collaborative law, arbitration, round table negotiations, and what happens if you do go to court.

If you're ready to talk to a solicitor, we'd like to invite you to a free, face-to-face meeting (valued at £200) with one of our expert family lawyers.

You can come to any of our offices, and make sure you find a solicitor who understands your individual needs and will look after your best interests.

Your future is in your hands. You can react to what happens to you… or you can choose to be proactive and take the lead to prevent any further anger or hurt.

Simply call us on 0800 999 4437 or email enquiries@parfittcresswell.com and book a time to come and tell us about your relationship.

Notes

Chapter 2

You Have Options: Alternative Dispute Resolution

You Don't Have To Go To Court To Get A Divorce

Many people believe a courtroom drama is an inevitable part of divorce. In fact, many couples can sort out the details of their separation together, or with the help of a professional, without needing to go through the difficulties and expense of court.

Unlike in the high-profile, sensational divorces you may hear about in the media, most people don't have knock-down, drag-out fights with their ex-partners.

Good family law solicitors believe court should be a last resort and most problems facing couples who are separating are best resolved without confrontation. Make sure you check your solicitor is a member of Resolution — an organisation of more than 6,500 family law professionals who believe most problems separating couples face are best solved without confrontation. Resolution provides advice, support, and training to family law solicitors. You can find a solicitor in your area by visiting www.resolution.org.uk/findamember/ — and if you search for our firm — Parfitt Cresswell — you'll find us in there too.

Divorce is always difficult, but resolving problems in a constructive, calm way leads to the most satisfactory, long-lasting outcomes for you and for any children.

It also makes it far more likely you'll be able to work amicably with your ex-partner after your divorce — which is crucial if you have children. It may even enable you to become friends eventually.

You have plenty of options — and in this chapter, we're going to explain them all to you. This is known as Alternative Dispute Resolution (ADR) and with the support of a professional, processes like this let you and your ex-partner talk through your problems together and work out what's best for you and your family.

There are several alternatives to court:

- Negotiation directly with your ex-partner or through a solicitor
- Mediation
- Mediation with a solicitor

- Collaborative law
- Family arbitration

All these processes give you privacy, allow you to control the pace, and — to a certain extent — you both control the outcome. In nearly all cases, you can choose to negotiate a settlement through your family lawyer *and* maintain an amicable relationship with your ex-partner.

Negotiation

Some couples find they can negotiate things for themselves at the end of a relationship. These are the lucky ones, and if you can manage to sit down with your partner and talk things through in a friendly manner, and come to an agreement, you should absolutely do that.

Whether you *can* do that will depend on how simple your issues are and whether you can comfortably talk about them.

Having said that, ending a relationship is at best emotional and at worst traumatic, so there is no shame at all if negotiating between yourselves is impossible.

Feelings run high and it's all too easy to get into an argument or lose your temper — and if you find that happening, it may be better to find a solicitor to negotiate on your behalf.

Even if you do sort things out between you, we strongly recommend you meet a solicitor once, just to make sure you've thought of everything. The last thing you want in your new life is for an ex-partner to be able to make a financial claim against you. We've seen this happen, even years after a divorce has been finalised.

Whatever you decide, it's really important to get legal advice because your solicitor can explain what the issues are, your rights, and how best to sort things out. An initial meeting on a fixed fee basis, so you know what to expect, can be a good place to start.

Whether you decide to negotiate between yourselves or ask solicitors to negotiate for you, you'll need to know where to start.

What's the First Step?

If you're asking a solicitor to negotiate your divorce and final settlement, you'll need to start by pulling together all your financial details in a financial disclosure. You can do much of this yourself, and your solicitor will be able to help you. There's a standard court form — called a Form E Financial Statement — that will help you do this.

When you or your solicitor has exchanged financial information with your ex-partner, you can ask your solicitor to negotiate on your behalf.

Your solicitor will look at all the options with you and help you understand how the law works and how the settlement can be structured. You'll want to find out what's the best you can achieve, and what would be unacceptable to you.

When you've done this, you can move onto the next steps, which are generally a combination of:

- Letters setting out proposals — a detailed starting point is helpful
- Telephone discussions, which can speed things up
- A face-to-face meeting involving everyone (although not necessarily at the same time)
- A 2-room meeting, which is more common when discussions are tense and emotional

Advantages of Solicitor Negotiation

Experienced family solicitors are very familiar with these types of negotiations, and will almost certainly have seen similar situations to yours before. They'll be able to explain what a fair settlement would be for you, and explain your options — then they'll be able to negotiate and achieve your goals, and get your divorce finalised and your financial settlement resolved.

Disadvantages of Solicitor Negotiation

It can become confrontational and make things more difficult between you and your partner, but a good family solicitor will make everything as simple, amicable, and painless as possible.

It can become expensive because most solicitors charge by time — and negotiations can drag on if you're not careful. You can ask if your solicitor can do fixed fees for negotiations, which may be possible for very simple cases.

Couples sometimes feel they're not in control of discussions about their financial settlement — but a good family solicitor should make sure you're fully involved and in control of everything throughout your divorce process.

Mediation

Mediation isn't about helping couples get back together; nor is it relationship counselling. Instead, it helps couples who are separating decide how to end their relationship and work things out together, whether that's how to make sure your children cope or to work out financial problems.

The mediator is there to make sure your discussion is constructive, non-combative, and that each of you is able to have your say.

During mediation, you and your ex-partner, helped by a trained mediator, will talk through the problems you need to solve. That might be money, children, property, business, or anything else affected by your separation. It's all about working out what's best for you and your children, if you have any.

Some describe mediation as like having a referee — or an impartial guide, if you prefer — for your discussions. Your mediator will be completely neutral and won't take sides, regardless of the circumstances of your separation — and they can't give advice. So most people going through mediation find it helpful to take advice and support from their family solicitor, who'll be able to make sure any agreements you reach during mediation are fair and legally binding.

Mediators can, however, give you information about the law and your options and draw up a Memorandum of Understanding setting out what you propose together. You can take it to your solicitor who can use it to work through all the legal steps you need to finalise your divorce.

Many couples say mediation helped them divorce or separate without increasing hostility and anger, and that discussing their problems face to face helped them reach fair solutions that suited them individually.

How Does It Work?

Before you start mediation, you'll each meet the mediator separately by phone or in person, to ensure you're both comfortable — and safe — to get together in discussions.

Traditionally, you'll have a number of sessions, each lasting about an hour and a half. You might need only one session, or you may need many; it depends on you and your partner, and what issues you're facing.

During the first session, you'll talk about the agenda and what issues you want to address. The mediator will help you gather information and to discuss your issues.

Why Go To Mediation?

Firstly, mediation really does help couples sort out issues and reach an agreement with as little stress, anguish, and strife as possible.

Secondly, it's by far the most cost-effective way of sorting out what happens when you split up.

You'll be involved in all the discussions, so you know when you get an agreement that it will be one you and your ex-partner can live with. You're in charge, and you'll find it's an empowering process. Instead of putting all the responsibility into the hands of your solicitor, you'll be the one driving the process. You'll be gathering the information you need and making sure you understand it.

If you go to court decisions will be made *for* you, and you'll have to live with them whether you like them or not. If you and your ex-partner can take control and work together amicably, though, *you* can make the decisions — and ensure they're the best ones for you and your family.

Is Mediation Compulsory?

No, it's not. We believe it's the right thing for most people to consider, as do most solicitors. So does the Government.

But it's not necessarily suitable for everyone, because you have to trust your ex-partner to be open and honest, especially when it comes to producing financial information. Some people are simply not reasonable, and it's difficult to get them to agree to things.

You also need to feel safe in mediation, so it's generally not appropriate if there is any domestic violence, abuse, or too much of a power imbalance in your relationship.

Before court proceedings can be issued, about children or money, you usually have to go to a Mediation Information and Assessment Meeting (MIAM) to make sure you know about the process. However, your solicitor may decide with you that a MIAM is unnecessary — perhaps because of domestic violence, or some aspect of extreme urgency.

You may also find mediation is inappropriate if you've already been through the collaborative law process and not been successful.

Of course, you also need to make sure your ex-partner is willing to go to mediation with you. You can't force someone to go if they don't want to — even if it's the best way forward. Don't push too hard if they're unwilling. You may find them more open to the idea as more time passes.

You can help by passing on as much information as you can about mediation. You could even give them a copy of this book — just get in touch with us and we'll send you another copy.

Mediation with a Solicitor

You might be thinking mediation sounds like a daunting prospect — something you don't want to do alone. In most cases, most people find mediation to be incredibly helpful… but you do have another option: lawyer-assisted mediation.

If your issues are very complex and there's a lot at stake, you can have your solicitor there during the sessions and take advice on the spot, or negotiate with your solicitor's help.

People often use lawyer-assisted mediation when court proceedings have already started, to sort out any issues without the expense and unpleasantness of being in a court room. This is called "shuttle mediation" and the idea is to produce a settlement when all else has failed.

If you choose this option, you should be aware it will be more expensive because your solicitors are there — however, if you have difficult legal issues it should be considered an investment rather than a cost. Going to court will inevitably cost far more.

Like all mediation, lawyer-assisted mediation is very flexible — but it's different from "normal" mediation because it tends to take place over one long session rather than over a series of shorter meetings.

The mediator is in charge and directs you and your solicitor, and your ex-partner and their solicitor.

You may have an initial meeting, then each meet separately with your solicitor and the mediator to work out what you want to achieve and what you're willing to agree to.

If that goes well, the mediator will bring everyone back together again to go through it all — and, if possible, your solicitors can draw up the agreement there and then.

Collaborative Law

Collaborative law is another way to deal with legal issues when a relationship breaks down. You'll each appoint your own solicitor, but instead of negotiating with your partner by letter or phone, you all get together to work things out.

As with mediation, the idea is to avoid going to court.

If you want to go down this route, make sure the solicitor you choose is properly trained, because it's a specialist area — not all solicitors can do it.

When you and your partner have decided with your solicitors to use collaborative law, your solicitor will set up your first four-way meeting — involving you, your partner, and your two solicitors.

You'll want to discuss with your solicitor what you'll need to do to prepare for your first meeting. Every family is different, so discussions will vary and some issues may be more urgent than others.

Before the meeting, your solicitors will talk to each other either in person or over the phone, and plan the meeting. They may also set an agenda so everyone knows what's going on. You and your partner will have input into the agenda and your solicitors will guide you.

Your First Four-Way Meeting

At your first four-way meeting, the solicitors will make sure you both understand you're committing to working out an agreement without going to court.

You'll probably both be asked to sign a Collaborative Participation Agreement — and it's important you understand the implications of this.

When you, your partner, and your solicitors have signed the agreement, you and your partner are committed to working things out without court. If you don't manage to resolve things during this process, you will not be able to instruct your current solicitors to issue court proceedings. If it all goes wrong, you'll have to instruct new lawyers, with all the extra expense that brings.

The good thing about a Collaborative Participation Agreement, though, is you can be confident your solicitors will do all they can to avoid you having to resort to expensive court proceedings.

Anchor Statements

One of the first things you'll be asked to do as part of the collaborative law process is write an anchor statement, which will be included in the minutes of your meetings.

You'll discuss anchor statements at your first or second four-way meeting. An anchor statement is simply a brief summary of why you've both chosen the collaborative process — and it gives you an opportunity to highlight what's important to you.

Anchor statements can sometimes be difficult to write — but they can have a big impact on how the collaborative process works.

The whole idea is to get you to focus on what you want to achieve from the collaborative process. They're long-term aims and may include some of the following wish-list items:

- To carry on parenting your children together
- Your children feel comfortable inviting both parents to their graduation, wedding, or other big family event
- To continue socialising with mutual friends
- To keep in touch with your parents-in-law
- To feel, for your own self-esteem, that you've been fair and conducted yourself with dignity throughout your separation process

These are some of the long-term aims our clients have put into their anchor statements in the past — you may have your own reasons for choosing collaborative law.

It can be difficult to focus on the future when you're concerned with immediate anxieties and emotions — but that's why anchor statements are so helpful. They help you keep a happy, calm, and productive future in sight when things seem very difficult.

If you're struggling to write your own anchor statement, you might want to consider these questions:

1. When you look back at this time ten years from now, what memories would you like to have?

2. What is the best possible outcome you could hope for, for the whole family — including your partner?

3. What do you want to avoid?

4. What really matters to you?

5. What does life look like for you in 12 months time?

Usually, you and your partner will read out your anchor statement at the first four-way meeting. This may happen before or after you sign the Collaborative Participation Agreement. Don't be surprised if one or both of you has an emotional reaction to this — it's perfectly normal and your solicitor will be expecting it.

The collaborative process provides a safe and supportive place for your discussions, and it does allow enough time for emotional moments.

Your solicitors may share their own anchor statements by explaining clearly why they've chosen to work collaboratively.

In later meetings, if you and your partner hit an obstacle or your discussions become heated and focused on short-term positions, it can be helpful to park those riskier discussions and go back to your anchor statements. That way, you can both focus on your long-term goals and move away from the immediately painful emotions.

Anchor statements are valuable when it comes to signing documents at your final meeting. You can both reflect on your initial aims and goals, and make sure the agreement you've reached is the best one for both of you.

How Many Meetings Will I Need?

The short answer to this question is: we don't know. You can't always predict how many meetings you'll need — it all depends on how much progress you make, how much common ground you have, and how many issues (and how complicated they are) you have to resolve.

In some cases, other professionals may need to get involved — like pension specialists, or financial planning advisors. If you have children, you might want someone trained in helping children to cope with divorce to be involved.

If emotions are affecting your discussions, you may find a family counsellor very helpful. Sometimes, a family counsellor can be far more cost-effective than a solicitor in resolving problems.

For example, you and your partner may both have the same goal when it comes to spending time with the children — but you find arranging the practicalities difficult. A family counsellor may be able to help you to reach an amicable solution — and may be able to give you techniques to use to avoid any future disagreements.

The Final Meeting

It's common (but not essential) to set up a final meeting when you've reached an agreement so you, your partner, and your lawyers can sign any Consent Order or Separation Agreement.

It also gives you the opportunity to talk through anything else that comes up — and gives you the opportunity to ask your solicitors to explain anything you don't fully understand, and talk you through the implications of what you've agreed.

For example, if you need to sell the family home, you might not be able to agree a firm timetable — but a final meeting will allow you to understand and clarify what happens next.

How Long Will the Collaborative Process Take?

Anywhere between four and 12 months is average.

One of the biggest benefits of this process is it's not driven by a timetable imposed by the court — so you can often resolve things much more quickly.

You and your partner have a lot of influence over how long everything takes, especially if you plan your meetings as far in advance as you can.

Remember: getting four busy people in one place can be tricky — especially if you and your partner face restrictions as to when you can meet.

Family Arbitration

Family arbitration is another method of resolving disputes at the end of a relationship.

A third party, called a family arbitrator, will make a decision about your finances for you. Just like a courtroom judge, a family arbitrator makes sure relevant facts and evidence are collected so they can make a fair decision.

The arbitrator will also consider the views of you and your partner when making a decision — but their decision, known as an "award", is final.

Family arbitration is an alternative to court proceedings and is used when a couple cannot resolve financial disputes. You might want to consider it if you and your partner have been unable to come to an agreement through discussions, or through collaborative law, mediation, or negotiations between lawyers.

You or your partner can suggest arbitration, but you both have to agree to it, to go ahead. Once you've appointed a family arbitrator, though, you can't back out of it without your partner's agreement.

You both choose the arbitrator, usually based on advice from your solicitor — or you can ask the Institute of Family Law Arbitrators (IFLA) to choose one for you.

It's a very flexible process — the only rule is your chosen arbitrator must apply the family law of England and Wales.

If you've chosen to use arbitration to deal with the finances during divorce, that's the only thing your family arbitrator will deal with. Other issues, like the process of ending the marriage, or contact with children, will be sorted out separately.

You should keep in mind that family arbitration means a decision is made for you — so it's like going to court in that respect. You shouldn't even be thinking about it until you've tried to sort out your finances by agreement, so do consider mediation or collaborative law first.

If you really can't agree everything and are choosing between court and arbitration, this section should help you decide.

Advantages of Family Arbitration

- You can choose an arbitrator with the experience to deal with your issues, so you know who you're getting. At court, you can't choose the judge and not every judge is a family law specialist. Family arbitrators have to be.

- Your arbitrator will deal with every stage of the process, so it's consistent — and you don't have to keep explaining the same things over and over again to a different judge, as may happen in court proceedings.

- You can choose exactly what you want your arbitrator to decide on — everything in dispute between you or one or two specific issues. For example, you might agree the amount of maintenance but not how long it should be paid for. Or you may argue about selling the house now or sometime in the future.

- You can agree on how to disclose your financial position to each other. You can use the same form as in court proceedings, but you don't have to. If you prefer, you could use a spreadsheet or piece of paper. Every case is different, and the arbitration process is a lot more flexible than court so you can choose whatever method works best for you. You could even agree to have the family arbitrator decide everything based on written evidence and representations rather than hearings.

- You can choose, with the arbitrator, where and when you meet. You're not stuck with court-imposed times.

- It's often much quicker than going to court. Court delays are becoming worse and worse — and in many parts of the country you can wait many months or even a year or more from the start to the finish of your case.

- Arbitration is much easier to keep private — there's no risk of journalists being present and confidential paperwork floating around a court.

What About the Disadvantages?

There aren't many disadvantages to arbitration, but you should consider:

- You must pay the family arbitrator's fees and you'll often have to pay extra to record each family arbitration hearing. If you were to go to court for the finances you'll have to pay court fees but you don't actually have to pay directly for a judge's time.

- The arbitrator cannot make an order to freeze assets or get assets back that have been wrongly removed.

If during your case there's a problem with your partner not being truthful about a financial position, or with assets being hidden or moved, then you can still go to court to put that right and then come back to arbitration.

However, if you believe at the start that this might happen court proceedings will probably be more appropriate.

What Can Family Arbitration Deal With?

Arbitration can deal with everything to do with family law finance including:

- Finances on divorce or civil partnership dissolution e.g. maintenance, property or pension sharing.

- Financial provision for children.

- Disputes between people who have been living together but are not married.

- Disputes between relatives about distributing someone's estate when they've died.

- Arbitration can also deal with some issues relating to children including:

  - Arrangements for children (e.g. where they live and how much time they spend with the other parent).

  - Relocation within England and Wales.

You can't use arbitration for serious disputes affecting children, like serious allegations or safeguarding, or international relocation.

These options aren't all-or-nothing: there's no reason why you and your partner can't choose arbitration to deal with one or two issues, but choose other methods for other problems.

For example, you might be in mediation, but have a problem with one or two simple issues. In that case, you could ask an arbitrator to decide rather than go to court — then come back to mediation to tie everything up.

Who's Involved in Arbitration?

The only people who must be involved are you, your partner, and the arbitrator.

But you or the arbitrator could involve others if appropriate. You can represent yourself, or ask your solicitor to help and advise you.

If assets like a property or company must be valued, or pensions are involved, the arbitrator can ask for expert evidence from a qualified professional. Arbitration is similar to court proceedings, so your solicitor may be able to represent your case and the legal arguments that support your position in the most cost-effective way.

Is An Arbitration Award Binding?

Yes. You and your partner agree at the start that you'll accept the decision whether you like it or not.

Technically, a court could override the decision — but in practice that won't happen unless there's a very good reason, like dishonesty in financial disclosure.

After the arbitrator has made the decision (award) in almost every case you'll ask the court to confirm it in a formal court order. This is really important, because if your partner doesn't comply with it, you need to be able to enforce it. It's essential if the decision involves sharing a pension.

You have only a limited right to appeal against the arbitrator's decision, so make sure this is the right decision for you.

How Much Does Arbitration Cost?

Costs will vary because each family is very different. But there are some things that affect costs:

- How much the arbitrator charges — which varies depending on their experience and where in the country you live. Most charge by the hour because it's difficult to estimate how long a case will take. Others may agree a fixed fee in simple cases.

- Venue: many arbitrators have their own premises and the venue will be covered in their hourly or fixed fees. Others will need to find a separate venue, so the cost will depend on where it is, and how many hearings you need.

- If you have the hearings recorded or transcribed, you'll need to pay those costs too.

Make sure you ask the arbitrator how the costs are likely to add up so you can budget properly. You should agree with your partner how to manage costs — and if you don't agree, you'll usually each pay your own costs. Remember, though, the arbitrator can make an order for one of you to pay some or all of the other's costs.

Because the process is usually much quicker than going to court, you'll save money there — but you'll have to pay separately for any court fees for the divorce process itself, or for turning the arbitrator's award into a formal court order.

You should also be aware you won't be able to get legal aid for arbitration.

What if We Go to Court?

Sometimes, it's impossible for couples to reach any kind of agreement. It's rare, but it does happen.

In that case, you or your ex-partner must apply to the court for what's known as a Financial Orders Application. This bit of legal jargon simply refers to the process of sorting out finances at the end of a relationship.

You'll both need to submit your financial statements (Form E), together with financial documents like bank statements, house valuations, and pension statements, and swear to them being true.

You both attend the first appointment in front of a district judge, who'll decide what directions are required — what you and your ex-partner need to do before the next meeting. Directions often include providing more information about your finances and which parts of the statement should be answered, or answered in more detail. They'll usually want justification for why certain claims should be considered and others should not, and part of this will decide which documents each of you should produce to support your statements.

If either of you refuses to cooperate, the court may take that to mean you have something to hide — so, as always, it's in your best interests to be totally honest and transparent.

The judge will also decide if you need to file any more evidence.

After this process, you'll go onto the financial dispute resolution hearing (FDR), which is judge-led mediation and your opportunity to settle things through negotiation and discussion.

Financial Dispute Resolution Hearing

You and your ex-partner should arrive at least an hour before the FDR starts so your solicitors can negotiate. The judge will have read all the paperwork, so during the hearing he/she will hear your solicitors' submissions and give you an idea as to the appropriate outcome. If your expectations are unreasonable, this part is very important — especially if one of you wants to "take 'em to the cleaners". In the vast majority of divorces, it's extremely unrealistic to aim to take *all* of an ex-partner's assets.

During the negotiations at FDR, the judge will see you and your solicitor to discuss any issues as many times as they can accommodate you throughout the day. If the court runs out of time when you're close to an agreement, the FDR can be adjourned (postponed until a later date).

Remember, even if you can't reach an agreement, your solicitor can still carry on negotiating on your behalf out of court. If you can reach an agreement this way, you can take things back to court at any time to get a consent order.

If you do reach an agreement at court, you and your partner or your solicitors will draft a consent order setting out the terms of the agreement. The judge will then consider the agreement and if he or she is satisfied the agreement is reasonable, they will seal the order, meaning it's binding on you and your partner.

If you can't reach an agreement — for whatever reason — the district judge will list the matter for a final hearing.

The Final Hearing

At the final hearing, you'll give evidence in the form of statements, then you and your partner will both give evidence in person.

If necessary, experts and witnesses will also give oral evidence at this point.

The judge at a final hearing will always be different from the judge who attended your FDR hearing. When this judge has heard all the evidence, they'll make a final order.

Of course, you and your ex-partner may still reach a financial settlement at any point during all these hearings — and if you do, your solicitors will draw up a consent order setting out the terms of your agreement. It will state it's the final settlement of all financial claims one of you has against the other.

It's filed at court, together with a form setting out all relevant assets and income, and the judge will consider it.

If it's a reasonable settlement, they'll approve it and make it an order, which will be binding on you and your partner.

How Long Will A Court Case Take?

How long it takes will depend on how willing you both are to cooperate and negotiate, and how complex your financial issues are.

If you can reach an agreement quickly, it will take much less time to finalise everything. If you can't reach an agreement, the whole court process can take up to a year or more until the final hearing.

Many family matters that reach the courts are based on both parties' needs. The court will consider how much money is available, and then consider the needs of you, your ex-partner, and your children (if you have any).

The money will be divided to make sure everyone's basic needs are met as far as possible, taking into account factors like employment. For example, if one parent is a full-time carer, they won't be able to take a permanent full-time job.

This is a very pragmatic, common-sense approach that leaves emotions out of it as much as possible.

Most cases settle long before a final hearing — but we, and all the solicitors at Parfitt Cresswell, always work with our clients to make sure final hearings never become a serious possibility unless it's unavoidable. It may be unavoidable if your partner refuses to engage in the court process or fails to provide information about their finances. Or, they may not be willing to accept or propose a reasonable settlement to allow you to reach an amicable agreement.

Summary

- Negotiation is ideal — especially if you can sort things out between yourselves, amicably, only working with a solicitor to check things over.

- Mediation is not about helping you get back together, it's about helping you decide how to end your relationship and work out financial problems or decide what's best for any children.

- Mediation with a solicitor gives you the added security of knowledgeable and experienced advice and help at every stage.

- Collaborative law aims to keep you out of court, too: you'll get together in a four-way meeting with your ex-partner and your solicitors, and work everything out together.

- Family arbitration involves someone else making your financial decisions for you. You have less control over things than in negotiations or mediation, but it will keep you out of court if you're finding it difficult to come to an agreement — and you get to choose the arbitrator.

- Court should be a last resort for those who find it impossible to work together or who have very complex financial issues. It could take a year or more to get to a final hearing — so we strongly recommend you try to avoid this at all costs.

In Chapter 3, we'll explain how to keep your divorce costs as low as possible, and talk about your funding options, so you can pay for your divorce — even if you're struggling.

Notes

Chapter 3

Keeping Costs Under Control

How to pay for your divorce, even if you're struggling

It's universally acknowledged that going through a divorce is one of the most stressful times in a person's life.

As if the emotional fallout of a relationship ending wasn't enough, you also have to deal with the financial, practical, and legal consequences.

Talking to a solicitor to get advice about likely outcomes and navigate the process is a great first step. Costs are likely to be high on your list of concerns at this point, so this chapter is full of practical advice about how to keep your costs as low as possible.

Hold Your Head High

Although it's tempting, it won't help you to bury your head in the sand and pretend this isn't happening. We're afraid it is, and facing it and dealing with it now will be far less stressful in the long run.

Getting good legal advice early on can help you identify any potential problems and show you how you can manage them — meaning you'll avoid some common mistakes that can prove very expensive.

Mistakes such as:

- Agreeing a financial settlement that's not in your best interests.
- Removing the incentive for your partner to deal with financial matters because you've moved out of the family home.
- Setting a precedent for spousal maintenance by paying your partner more than you should.
- Increasing your chance of going to court because you refuse to agree to something which you *would* have agreed had you understood the legal implications.

A good family solicitor will make sure you understand all your options and avoid making such mistakes.

Lean On Your Support Network

You'll need help from your entire support network — family, friends, and professionals — to get through the breakdown of your relationship.

Friends and family will be a great source of comfort and support, and you should lean on them for that. Do not, however, use your friends or family as legal advisors. You'll probably know someone who's gone through a divorce and they may well be eager to help…

But no two families are the same and any financial settlement will depend on your individual circumstances. Your friends and family are perfect when you need a shoulder to cry on, or an ear to rant into, or a friendly face to just listen.

A trained counsellor will help you work through any emotional problems, and will be able to help you and your ex-partner get through any anger or mistrust.

A solicitor is there to help you understand the law, and make sure you don't make any costly mistakes. You don't *have* to instruct a solicitor to act for you, but for most people it's a very good idea. Even essential.

Bear in mind, though, that your solicitor will be charging you for their expertise in family law — they're not a substitute for friends, family, or counsellors. We do have a lot of practical advice that can help you, and many of us have been through divorces ourselves… but we're not trained counsellors.

Make sure you're only paying your solicitor for their legal expertise. You can find much more appropriate emotional and other support from counsellors, family, and friends.

If you're not sure who's the best person to help you with a particular question or problem, here are some of the most common questions we get:

Friend:

- "This is so unfair — how can my partner treat me this way?"
- Hugs and sympathy
- "I cannot believe this is the way the court system works! What about the fact he/she cheated on me / is refusing to see the children / etc.?"

Counsellor:

- "I don't know how to cope with him / her / life / proceedings / children."
- "I don't know how I'm going to be able to move on."

Solicitor:

- "I don't know how to deal with divorce."
- "What are my rights and obligations when it comes to the children?"
- "How much money am I likely to get when we get divorced?"
- "He / she has changed the locks — what do I do now?"

Choose Your Solicitor Wisely

Your solicitor will charge for their time and their hourly rate will depend on their experience... and on their location. (London lawyers will usually cost more than regional firms.)

If your divorce is complicated, you should consider working with a more experienced solicitor. Although their fees may seem too expensive, using a cheaper solicitor could cost you more in the long run, as their inexperience could lead to your divorce dragging on for longer than it should do.

If your divorce is pretty simple, though, you probably won't need to instruct a partner with 20+ years' experience and the matching hourly rate.

Many people feel very hurt and angry about the breakdown of their relationship, and feel like they want to "make them pay" or "take them to the cleaners". If you feel like this, you may be tempted to find a solicitor with a reputation for being a Rottweiler...

And there may be some situations in which this is an appropriate choice to make.

For most people, though, it's far better to put your trust in a specialist family solicitor who can help you resolve everything quickly, as painlessly as possible, and with minimal costs.

You should also encourage your ex-partner to seek early advice, because if you both get sensible legal advice you'll be more likely to agree on everything without needing to go to court.

When you're choosing your solicitor, it's really important for you to build a rapport with them — so when you meet or talk with them for the first time, make sure you feel comfortable with them or you'll find it difficult to work together.

It's worth putting a little time into finding the right solicitor at the start, because changing solicitors during your divorce will increase your costs.

If you can find a solicitor who offers a free initial consultation or a chat on the telephone before you actually get started, take them up on it. You'll be able to decide whether you've found the right solicitor — and they'll be able to make sure you're the right client and they can help you.

Stay Out Of Court If You Can!

Going to court is by far the most expensive (and unpleasant) way of getting divorced, and you should try your best to avoid it. A good specialist family solicitor will talk you through all the options available to you.

If you've read Chapter 2, you'll be familiar with your options and may even have an idea of how you and your ex-partner want to proceed.

Your solicitor should be able to help you save money, time, and heartache by avoiding long, drawn-out negotiations and arguments — an out-of-court settlement will almost certainly be less expensive.

Having said that, it's still important for you to reach an agreement as fast as you can — the longer it takes, the more time your solicitor will have to spend on your case, and the higher the fees will be. A good specialist solicitor will do their best to get everything wrapped up for you fast... whereas an inexperienced one may inadvertently make things much more difficult.

We once acted for a husband in his divorce, working with him to sort out financial matters. He'd transferred from another solicitor part-way through the process because he'd been with them for many months — but they'd made no progress.

We advised him to issue court proceedings and we were able to conclude the divorce and the financial matters within 4 months because we reached an agreement at the first court hearing.

He was a very happy client because it took less time to conclude than he'd spent with his previous lawyer going through a voluntary exchange of information.

An experienced lawyer can help you sort everything out much faster than you might think is possible — and that will help you keep your costs down.

Invest in Early Negotiation

The cliché "time is money" is very appropriate when it comes to legal costs — so if you can agree the division of assets and income without going through lengthy court proceedings, you'll save a lot of money.

Do Your Homework

As you no doubt know, solicitors charge depending on how much time they spend on your case. So the less time they spend dealing with your divorce, the less it will cost.

If your solicitor asks you for information, give it to them in an organised, comprehensive, and easy-to-read manner, because they'll be able to read through it much faster.

If you're not sure if something's relevant, include the information anyway — your solicitor can filter out anything they don't need to know when they're going through your paperwork. This will be quicker and cheaper than going backwards and forwards because they keep asking you for more information.

Don't hesitate to ask for more guidance about what they want from you — they'll be happy to spend a few minutes going through it with you, and it will save you money in the long run.

If your solicitor puts a deadline on any information they ask for, make sure you get it to them on time. If they need to chase you, they'll charge you for it and you may miss an important deadline — and if you're working under pressure, you're more likely to make mistakes.

The earlier you deal with this, the easier your solicitor will find your case and the lower their fees will be.

Be Truthful — And Try To Stay Friendly

Trust often breaks down at the same time as a relationship — and both partners can feel like they're being put under the microscope.

Although it may seem like you're under suspicion and being asked for more information than seems necessary, it's really important you provide as much information as you can. If financial disclosure on either side is incomplete, your solicitors will need to prepare detailed questionnaires — and that increases your legal costs.

Difficult though it may be, if you can stay on relatively friendly terms, you'll be much more likely to keep your costs down (as well as keeping any unpleasantness at a minimum).

This is important because there are several ways your ex-partner can increase *your* legal costs — including by acting contrary to the advice given in this book. There's nothing your solicitor can do to prevent your partner acting in such a way, and there are only very limited circumstances in which your ex-partner will be penalised, or even just criticised, by the courts.

The best way to avoid such a situation is for both of you to be as amicable as possible.

Principles Are Expensive

Your solicitor will instinctively undertake a cost-benefit analysis at the start, throughout the process, and especially when considering settlement proposals.

This does not mean your solicitor isn't fighting your corner; it means they're considering whether the benefit to *you* is outweighed by the cost of going after information or documents.

Arguing about a point of principle is unlikely to reap big financial rewards for you, so do consider your solicitor's advice very carefully.

Most divorces will reach a point in negotiations where you need to make a decision about whether to accept a settlement. No solicitor can guarantee an outcome at court so you'll want to think about whether you're likely to achieve a better outcome if you pursue things through the court — bearing in mind how much it will cost to get there.

Let us give you an example. If we tell you spending legal costs of £10,000 is likely to result in you receiving £20,000+ then it's worth pursuing.

However, if we tell you spending £10,000 is likely to result in you receiving £10,000, you don't gain anything.

And if we tell you spending £10,000 may or may not get you £10,000 you could end up losing out completely, and being out of pocket. Under those circumstances your solicitor may advise you against pursuing your point — even though it may be entirely valid.

This type of situation can stick in your craw, but we advise you to try to take your emotions out of the equation and consider if it's really worth it.

Letters and Phone Calls

There are many ways you can get in touch with your solicitor, but email and telephone are the most common. If you email or phone your solicitor every day with questions, your legal costs will definitely go up.

Our top tip for you is to make a note of your questions and comments every time they pop up, and then compile a list once a week. Email it to your solicitor, and they'll be able to consider everything at once and respond to you in one email — which will be much more cost-effective for you.

We've had clients who would send us an email, then telephone us immediately, just as the email popped up in the inbox. There's little point in speaking to that client until we've had time to read the information and/or questions — and find an answer.

We'll still need to read the email, but now it'll take longer.

If you want to know whether your solicitor has received a letter or sent something to you, try calling their secretary — it's unlikely you'll be charged for that. If you call the solicitor, you'll definitely be charged for it.

We solicitors have a reputation for charging for every second spent on cases... but the truth is, it's pretty simple to keep your costs down. We're not out for everything we can get, but we do need to use our time — and your time — wisely.

Funding Options

Separation and divorce can be a stressful and emotionally draining experience. One that can be made all the more stressful when worries of financial uncertainty race through your mind.

The fear of not being able to pay for legal representation during a divorce can often lead to many sleepless nights. It's the worry about paying solicitors' fees that leads many people to fend for themselves. Many assuming going without expert legal advice and representation is the only way they can proceed.

However, although going it alone might seem like your best — or even your only — option, it often isn't. Going it alone is not always the most cost-effective choice and representing yourself can actually mean your case takes longer. If you represent yourself, you may increase your chances of going to court — or you may find you don't reach as good a settlement as you could have with expert legal help.

You have several options to help you fund your divorce or separation. We'll go through them here.

Legal Aid

Unfortunately, since April 1, 2013, Family Law Legal Aid has been all but abolished by the Legal Aid and Prosecution of Offenders Act 2012. This Act effectively reduced the availability of Legal Aid to cases of domestic abuse, leaving many people fighting their own legal battles or looking for alternative solutions, like arbitration.

This has severely limited everyone's options — and it can have significant and damaging consequences. Legal Aid is still available if you've suffered domestic violence, but it's very limited.

Savings and Investments

Many people turn to savings and investments to pay for the cost of their divorce — but if your savings are held in a joint account, your ex-partner may object to you using them until a settlement is agreed.

Bank Loan

You can take out a bank loan for a fixed sum, to be repaid on a set date with a fixed APR. The downside is you would have to make your monthly repayments during the course of your separation and *before* you get a financial settlement or court order — so it may stretch your finances.

Legal Services Order

You can apply to the court for funds from your ex-partner to pay your legal fees. Remember, your ex must have enough income or assets for this method to be effective. There's no point applying for a court order if your spouse can't provide the necessary funding.

To obtain a legal services order, you'll have to prove this is the last resort for you and you have no other way of paying the legal costs for your divorce.

Credit Cards

This is an expensive source of finance if you don't clear the balance every month. Plus, of course, you have to repay a minimum amount each month, so it may not be suitable for some people.

You can still find 0% rates, but this is often only a short-term fix and may not be your best option. Problems also arise when you reach your credit card limit — but your legal costs continue to rise.

Borrowing from Family and Friends

Loans from family and friends are often called "soft loans". They're usually undocumented, with no interest charged, and with no set repayment date.

The court often doesn't take them into consideration when considering the overall financial position of you and your ex-partner, because such loans are often treated as a gift.

If you do borrow from friends or family, you could have a loan agreement drafted by a solicitor and signed by you and your lender — which could help to ensure the court takes your loan into account.

Remortgage Your Property

If there's enough equity in it, you could remortgage your property — but only if it's in your sole name, or both parties agree. This usually offers a low interest rate compared to credit cards.

Third-Party Loans

Companies like Novitas offer divorce litigation funding — but they may ask for security, such as a charge over your property. You should always get independent legal advice when you're considering this option.

Sears Tooth Agreement

This is an agreement between you and your solicitor in which you irrevocably agree to pay their fees out of your capital settlement at the end of your divorce case.

It allocates to your solicitor a portion of your financial settlement up to the value of your legal costs.

Most solicitors will not be willing to offer this type of agreement because it significantly increases the payment delay. There's also a risk of not being paid at all.

Working With Your Solicitor

One final point to note: solicitors are not allowed to enter into no-win no-fee conditional agreements in family law and you can't instruct them under similar terms to a personal injury lawyer. Nor are they lending institutions: solicitors won't wait to be paid from the assets when the divorce has been finalised.

Talk to your solicitor. Ask as many questions as you need to make sure you know what your solicitor thinks each stage of your divorce will cost.

Your solicitor should be completely open with you and should be able to give you a rough estimate of costs.

Agree from the start how and when you'll pay fees — and ask to receive regular cost updates. Your solicitor will not want you to struggle financially — it's not in your interests and it's not in their interests, either.

Summary

- Tempting though it is, burying your head in the sand will only prolong your divorce — and increase your costs. Instead, lean on your friends, family, counsellors — and take the advice your legal professional offers.

- Choose your solicitor wisely: someone who'll keep you out of court if you can, work in your best financial and personal interests, and whom you like.

- Do your homework, be truthful, and try to stay amicable — you'll get through everything far more quickly and far more cheaply.

- Be open about any funding concerns you have — talk to your solicitor about your options, and make sure you get estimates and regular cost updates so you can stay on top of your fees.

In Chapter 4, we'll look at the financial implications of getting divorced: your home, your pension, your salary, and your will.

Notes

Chapter 4

Making Sense of Finances

What happens to your assets and your business?

When you got married the law gave you and your spouse the right to make certain financial claims during a divorce. These include claiming a share of properties, capital (savings and investments), pension funds, and each person's income (i.e. maintenance payments).

The claims continue during marriage and after divorce unless you get a Court Order, either by agreement or imposed by the court, setting out the terms of your financial agreement. This court order will usually include a clause stating the claimant cannot make any further financial claims once the court order is implemented.

(This safeguards each spouse from future financial upheaval.)

All this sounds terribly complicated, especially when couched in such dense legal jargon — but it doesn't have to be. In this chapter, we're going to explain how financial settlements work and how they'll affect your family home, pensions, wills, savings and investments.

Remember: you can contact us for a free initial meeting at any time, and we'll make sure you understand all the implications for you and your family.

Financial Disclosure

The first thing you'll have to do when negotiating finances during a divorce is exchange full, frank, and clear financial disclosure with your ex-spouse. That means you'll have to open your books for your ex-spouse to look through.

We know it may seem like a huge invasion of privacy, but the fastest and cleanest way to settle your divorce amicably and move on is for you and your ex-spouse to exchange financial information and documents. Until you both know what each of you has in terms of capital, income, and pensions — and what their value is — you can't start negotiating on how to divide them between you.

The simplest way to do this is for you each to complete a Financial Statement (Form E), that's used in family court proceedings. You can each enter your information clearly and logically, and make sure you don't miss anything out. This makes it easy for you to compare and easy for you to account for all your assets.

It's really important you both include everything, or the financial agreement you reach may not be as fair or advantageous as you think, and could be set aside for misrepresentation or fraud.

When you're completing Form E, you'll both need to provide the following documents and evidence as a minimum:

- 12 months' bank statements
- Investment statements
- Recent house valuations
- Up-to-date mortgage statement
- Pension fund valuations
- Evidence of debts
- Your last three payslips
- Your P60

You may be able to agree with your ex-spouse to have a more limited exchange of financial disclosure. For example, if you believe you know your marital assets very well — including those in your ex-spouse's name — you might want to agree to provide just the last six months' bank statements.

Try to collate your financial information in a logical, focused manner so all your valuations are up to date. This will save you time and expense later on, because if your valuations were conducted too long ago, they'll be out of date and will need to be done again.

It's a good idea to get three valuations for your home and take the average as a base figure to work from when negotiating division of assets.

You'll also want to look at any investments you may have, which may include cash, stocks and shares, and other property. Most investments are divided based on the valuation figure, but some plans may have guarantees on maturity and/or penalties for cashing them in — so you should consider carefully how best to share them. In some cases you can assign a joint policy so when it matures the assignee will receive benefits.

Pensions always cause the most work and confusion during divorce settlements. Pension values or cash equivalents often don't represent the true value of the benefits the pension will pay, so you must look at them with caution. They're not necessarily the best basis to use for dividing the pension.

Most pension providers are familiar with valuations for divorce purposes and will give you a standardised response if you ask them. If your pension isn't yet being paid, the provider will give you one valuation per year free of charge (this normally relates to final salary pensions). If the pension is in payment, the provider usually charges for a valuation.

"What if someone disputes my financial disclosure?"

This is quite common during divorces, so you should be scrupulously honest about your finances — and be very diligent so you don't make any mistakes, either.

If anyone discovers you've been dishonest in any way, the court will take an extremely dim view of it and it may affect your final settlement. In extreme cases, it may be considered perjury — and that's very serious indeed.

If you suspect your spouse has been dishonest, you'll need to approach it carefully and you should discuss it with your solicitor. Once upon a time, if you'd discovered hidden assets through inappropriate means, like rooting through their possessions, for example, the court would accept that evidence.

But the law has changed and that evidence would not be admissible today.

If you suspect dishonesty, we recommend you bring it up during negotiations and if they don't come clean, or no evidence surfaces, you can apply to the court.

The court has a range of powers to force financial disclosure when one person is not being forthcoming, or where there's suspicion of dubious conduct. The court can issue orders to search properties and seize documents and disclosure orders against third parties.

Although the courts don't often use these methods at the moment, they're likely to become more common in future.

Considering a Financial Settlement

When you've both prepared your disclosure, you'll set a date to send each other's solicitor a copy of your Form E. Your solicitor will consider it carefully and prepare a schedule of the assets — and start looking at your options for dividing them.

Your solicitor should consult with you to find out what you want to achieve and whether it will be possible.

To make a suitable proposal to your ex-spouse, your solicitor will take into account S25 of the Matrimonial Causes Act 1973:

25. *Matters to which court is to have regard in deciding how to exercise its powers under ss. 23, 24 and 24A*
(1) It shall be the duty of the court in deciding whether to exercise its powers under section 23, 24 [24A or 24B] above and, if so, in what manner, to have regard to all the circumstances of the case, first consideration being given to the welfare while a minor of any child of the family who has not attained the age of eighteen.

(2) As regards the exercise of the powers of the court under section 23(1)(a), (b) or (c), 24 [24A or 24B] above in relation to a party to the marriage, the court shall in particular have regard to the following matters:-

(a) the income, earning capacity, property and other financial resources which each of the parties to the marriage has or is likely to have in the foreseeable future, including in the case of earning capacity any increase in that capacity which it would in the opinion of the court be reasonable to expect a party to the marriage to take steps to acquire;

(b) the financial needs, obligations and responsibilities which each of the parties to the marriage has or is likely to have in the foreseeable future;

(c) the standard of living enjoyed by the family before the breakdown of the marriage;

(d) the age of each party to the marriage and the duration of the marriage;

(e) any physical or mental disability of either of the parties to the marriage;

(f) the contributions which each of the parties has made or is likely in the foreseeable future to make to the welfare of the family, including any contribution by looking after the home or caring for the family;

(g) the conduct of each of the parties, if that conduct is such that it would in the opinion of the court be inequitable to disregard it;(© Crown copyright)

All that legalese essentially means the court will decide whether or not to exercise its powers, and if so, how it will make its decision. They'll always put children first — and they'll take into consideration all the points listed from (a) to (g).

Your solicitor will also consider any case law — which means they'll look at what judgements and decisions judges in higher courts have made in the past. This gives us an idea as to what you could expect as a reasonable settlement.

The case law we have at the moment makes it clear that a judge should try to reach a fair outcome based on factors (a) to (g) listed above. How important each factor is in the decision will depend on your personal situation.

Courts will always start by considering what the settlement would look like if your net assets were divided equally — and will only depart from equality if there are good reasons to do so, most commonly due to "needs of the parties". The needs of children are always a court's first consideration.

Assets are often *not* split equally, and the law allows a wide discretion to enable the court to make an order, or for you and your ex-spouse to reach a settlement that's reasonable and fair to both of you. Your solicitor will be able to advise you about your specific settlement options.

"What Will Happen to Our Family Home?"

Dividing the family home can be quite simple. It's often possible to sell the home so you can buy two smaller ones (as long as you can get mortgages if you need to). So when you've sold your property, the money will be divided between you and your ex-spouse, based on your incomes and mortgage capacities.

Sometimes, one spouse may keep the family home for themselves and the children. This may mean transferring ownership solely to one spouse.

If the court decides it's not appropriate to sell the property immediately, but an outright transfer of ownership is unfair to the other person, there may be a deferred trust. This means one spouse and the children can live there until the children reach a certain age, or other specified event, at which point the property is sold. The proceeds will be divided as agreed.

There are other options, too. The property may be sold when the occupying spouse leaves, remarries, or dies.

Or the family home may be transferred into the sole name of the person living there, who grants a charge to their ex-spouse to reflect their interest.

"What will happen to my pension?"

Your pension is one of your most valuable assets — but it's often neglected during a divorce. There are three possible ways to deal with it:

1. Adjust the marriage assets to account for pension rights, offsetting them against other assets.

2. Earmark a proportion of the pension and lump sum for your ex-spouse, for them to receive in future when your pension is in payment.

3.   Split the pension so it's divided when you divorce, effectively creating two separate pension funds you can both contribute to in future (a pension sharing order).

The court doesn't have to make a pension sharing order, but it must still take pensions into account when looking at financial settlements.

You should also be aware that just because your pension was subject to an order from a previous marriage, doesn't mean it's safe during a second divorce!

"Will I get maintenance from my ex-spouse?"

This is a question we're asked often and the answer is that it depends on several things. If there's a significant disparity between yours and your ex-spouse's incomes and future earning capacities, the court can seek to address this in any agreement. This can be by way of a capital adjustment in favour of the lower earner or by way of ongoing spousal maintenance payments.

The test which the court must apply is to assess the level of maintenance required to be paid (if any) together with the payer's ability to pay that or any amount of maintenance, without affecting that person's ability to meet their own needs. It's a balancing act.

If there are children, the court will always look at child maintenance before calculating spousal maintenance. It may be that after paying child maintenance, there's nothing left over to pay spousal maintenance.

In middle to high-income families, there's usually more money available, so the court will ensure the family's needs are met, then consider their accustomed standard of living before deciding what (if any) spousal maintenance should be paid.

You can read more about the finer details of maintenance below.

"How will a divorce affect my will?"

You should have an up-to-date will to make sure your estate (all your assets) are handled as you wish after you die — but if you're getting divorced, you'll need to go back to your will to make sure it still does what you want it to.

Contrary to what some believe, getting divorced won't void or invalidate your will. Instead, when your divorce is finalised, any provisions in your will which benefit your ex-spouse are automatically revoked.

That simply means that for all intents and purposes, your ex-spouse will be treated as if they are dead. They won't inherit your estate once your decree absolute (or decree of dissolution in a civil spouseship) has been made.

Of course, that may be what you want — but if you'd left *everything* to your ex-spouse, it's particularly important you go back and revise your will, because the effect is as if you'd died without a will at all, which will complicate things for those left behind.

Similarly, if you appointed your ex-spouse as your executor, that role will automatically be revoked when your divorce is finalised — even if you'd appointed them trustee of a trust for the benefit of your children.

However, if you were to die before your divorce was finalised, your ex-spouse would receive any gifts or provisions you left to them. For that reason, it may be best to make a new will as soon as you decide to separate — so everyone is clear about what happens when you die.

Perhaps the most important thing to ensure, though, is any money you want to leave to your children will go to them no matter what. It's vital that if you want your children to be sure of an inheritance, you leave it to them specifically.

Let's say your ex-spouse remarries in future. Anything they take into the relationship is considered theirs to use, which means if they divorce a second time, anything they've inherited will be subject to the second lot of divorce proceedings — which means money you intended for your children may instead go to their new spouse as part of the divorce settlement.

Far too many people fail to consider this during a divorce — but we strongly advise you to think about it and *act* on it as soon as you possibly can — even if a new spouse hasn't come into the picture yet.

"What Can We Claim For?"

When you're getting divorced, the court can make income orders and capital orders and these fall into four financial areas you can claim for:

1. Property Adjustment Orders

2. Capital Lump Sum Orders

3. Pension Sharing / Attachment Orders

4. Periodical Payment and Secured Periodical Payment. Maintenance Orders for spouse and/or child

Your solicitor will be able to explain what each of these means for you.

Maintenance Orders

Spousal Maintenance

Every spouse has the right to make a claim for maintenance, but that doesn't guarantee you'll receive a spousal maintenance order.

In most cases, the purpose of maintenance is to make sure both spouses can meet their daily outgoings. It isn't about simply equalising two different incomes.

It's important for both spouses to have a relatively similar standard of living and meet their reasonable needs — which is what financial settlements are all about.

When we talk about income, we mean all forms of income — including employment and self-employment, any state benefits you may receive, rental income, investments like dividends and pensions, and income from a business.

There's no statutory formula for calculating spousal maintenance. It's really a two-stage test.

Firstly, the court must consider the lower earner (often the wife) and assess her total income from all sources, her reasonable outgoings, and whether there's a deficit (outgoings are more than income).

A spousal maintenance order should be considered if she has more money going out than coming in. If that's the case, the court will focus on the higher earner and decide, on the basis of their income and outgoings, if they can meet or reduce their spouse's deficit.

The court can make the following orders — either by an agreed consent order or by imposing a court order during court proceedings:

1.   Monthly payments from one spouse to another.

2.   Nominal maintenance payments from one spouse to the other.

3.   A one-off lump sum payment instead of monthly payments.

4.   A clean break order dismissing all claims for maintenance.

When the court makes an order for monthly spousal maintenance payments, it will specify the exact amount and the exact date — for example, £500 per month, to be paid on the 1st of each month, to start on April 1, 2017.

The order will also specify how long the payments will continue — and there are two options:

1. For joint lives — meaning until either spouse dies, or the receiving spouse remarries.

2. For a defined term — e.g. Until the youngest child reaches age 18, or completes secondary education, or graduates from university... or for a fixed period, say five years.

If you're awarded a spousal maintenance order and you get married again, you'll automatically no longer be entitled to those payments — and your right to claim against your ex-spouse will be dismissed.

Unlike a capital lump sum order, maintenance orders can be varied depending on changing circumstances. Let's look at a few examples:

If the receiving spouse returns to work or gets a pay rise, maintenance could be decreased.

If the paying spouse loses their job by redundancy or ill health, maintenance could be decreased or dismissed.

If a specific termination clause was included by agreement — for example if the receiving spouse lives with a new spouse for more than 6 months.

If you haven't agreed (or been ordered by the court) that maintenance will stop when a specific event happens (such as living with a new spouse), the paying spouse may ask to decrease the payment — or dismiss the claim altogether.

Any term can be extended by agreement or by court order, unless the court makes an order that it shall be "non-extendable". This means if an order is made for payments to stop five years from the date of the court order, and it shall be non-extendable, the receiving spouse has no right to ask their ex-spouse or the court to increase the time limit at any time.

A nominal Spousal Maintenance Order means that no monies change hands but the claim for maintenance remains open and potentially variable upwards for the duration of the agreed term. It is often considered as a required safety net where there are young children.

If you receive a one-off lump sum, it's called a capitalisation of your claim. This means you don't have the right to pursue any future maintenance payments from your ex-spouse and your maintenance claim is dismissed. You've already received the money upfront as a cash sum instead.

Finally, if the court decides you should *not* receive spousal maintenance, either because you can't demonstrate a need, your income positions are roughly comparable, or your spouse simply can't afford to make any payments — you'll agree or the court will order your claims to be dismissed. This is a "clean break".

Child Maintenance

As both parents are responsible for the costs of raising children the absent parent will be required to contribute to the cost of the child's care. This usually means regular financial payments to the parents with care. You and your ex-spouse agree this in a family-based agreement, through the Child Maintenance Service or by court order.

Family-based agreements are often easiest to arrange, but if the agreement breaks down you won't be able to enforce it because it isn't legally binding.

The Child Maintenance Service is a Government scheme which started in 2012 and replaced the Child Support Agency. It's available for you if you're unable to reach a family agreement, if your agreement has broken down, or if you just want the certainty of having a legally enforceable agreement. There is a fee for using the service.

Court Order for Child Maintenance

A court can deal with child maintenance in certain circumstances where:

- Your ex-spouse lives abroad and you can't use the Child Maintenance Service.

- Your ex-spouse is a high earner and has a gross income of more than £3,000 per week (sum correct at time of publication). The receiving ex-spouse can apply for top-up maintenance in addition to any award under the Child Maintenance Service.

- You wish to apply for payment of school or university fees.

- For step children.

- To meet the costs of a child's disability.

- For a child who has left secondary education.

Child maintenance is a complicated area and varies depending on your circumstances. It's worth speaking to a family lawyer to make sure you understand what options are available to you.

The Consent Order

When you've finished negotiations and you've reached a full and final financial settlement with your spouse, it's time to formalise it all with a consent order.

A consent order is the legal document that sets out the terms of the financial agreement you've reached. For the consent order to be made into an order, it must go to the court so a district judge can consider it.

Don't worry — you don't need to attend court in person because your solicitor will submit the consent order by post as a paper application.

When the judge considers the financial agreement, he/she will refer to a Statement of Information for Consent Order form. This form summarises your financial circumstances. It's basically a short version of Form E, which enables the judge to see if the agreement is fair and reasonable based upon all the circumstances of the case and the s25 factors we referred to above.

The court does not have to approve and seal the consent order if it's concerned about the division of assets. The judge must be satisfied the agreement is fair and reasonable and that it meets everyone's needs based on the facts. The court can raise questions about the consent order until it's satisfied — and only then will the judge seal the consent order to create a legally binding and enforceable court order.

The Court Order

When the court makes an order, the agreement is legally binding and all the financial claims a couple can make against each other will be satisfied or dismissed. This means that neither of you has a right to renegotiate the terms or apply to the court for further claims, unless it relates to an open claim. It's usually only claims for spousal maintenance that remain open.

This means both spouses must comply with the terms in the court order, and if either one refuses to do so, the other can apply to the court to enforce and implement anything that was supposed to happen.

For example, if a jointly owned property was ordered to be transferred into the sole name of one spouse, but the other refuses to sign the transfer deed, they can apply to the court for a short hearing. The judge has the power to execute and sign the transfer deed on behalf of the other spouse so the transfer of ownership of the property can complete. If a court order hadn't been obtained in the first place, this wouldn't be possible.

Your Options

When you start divorce proceedings, your solicitor will talk to you about the different options you have open to you — so you can decide how you want to deal with your financial discussions.

These are the options we talked about in Chapter 2 — including what happens if you have to go to court.

What's Next?

After the consent order has been sealed by the court, or a court order has been made, you need to implement the terms.

Your divided assets will naturally be worth less than your joint assets — and it can be rather daunting to work out what are the next steps after your divorce, particularly if you don't have a solicitor. Here are a few of the more common steps...

You'll have to move any agreed pension share from one fund to another — which can be confusing because there are so many options.

You'll have to sort out another mortgage if you're buying a new property, or even remortgage your current home.

And you'll probably want to discover how best to use the assets and cash you're left with.

We would strongly recommend you get in touch with a financial advisor who specialises in divorce and post-

divorce finances to help you make sense of what's left —
and to help you plan for a brighter future.

The sooner you do this — preferably early on during
your divorce process — the better prepared you'll be not
just to cope with the divorce, but to make the most of
what you have afterwards.

A Client's Story

Our client had been separated from her husband for five
years when she was able to buy him out of their former
marital home, where she lived with the children. When
she came to us, she'd been trying to speak with her
estranged husband, and also his parents, who had a
charge secured against the house.

We hoped they could reach an agreement as to how
much her ex-spouse and his parents would receive, so
they could remove their interest in the property.
Unfortunately, he refused to negotiate, and remained
silent.

This left our client with no option but to start
Financial Remedy proceedings through the court. Her
husband failed to respond to many letters we'd sent, and
he also failed to comply with the court's instructions and
attend the first hearing.

At that hearing, the district judge ordered that unless
our client's husband complied with the court's
instructions, he would transfer the whole equity in the
house to the wife, subject to the mortgage and his parents'

interest, both of which would obviously need to be repaid. Perhaps surprisingly, her husband still failed to act, so at the next hearing the court made an order to transfer her husband's interest in the property to our client, together with an order for costs against the husband. This allowed our client to recover a substantial amount of her court costs.

This is not at all the result our client had imagined. However, having brought the courts into it, she was able to argue her case, and get a far better result than she had originally hoped to achieve.

Summary

- It's vital that you and your ex-partner are scrupulously honest about your finances when it comes to financial disclosure. If you're not, it will slow things down and increase expenses at best — and could be considered perjury at worst.

- The family home, pension, and any savings and investments are all likely to be divided up when you get divorced — but individual financial circumstances will dictate what happens. The court always has fairness in mind.

- You'll only get maintenance from a spouse if there's enough left in the pot after any child maintenance has been calculated, and if income exceeds outgoings.

- Do not neglect your will! It won't become void on your divorce, so you need to make sure it still reflects your wishes — especially if you have children.

Chapter 5 is all about business — so if you're a business owner, or your ex-spouse owns a business, you should read it carefully.

Notes

Chapter 5

Attention Business Owners!

Keeping your business secure after your divorce

If you own a family business you might assume your business will be protected during your divorce… but that's not always the case. Businesses used to be protected during a divorce but this has changed — and the family business is now considered a matrimonial asset and will need to be disclosed during financial disclosure.

There are few things worse for a business than the owner getting divorced because the business itself is likely to be subject to an in-depth forensic analysis. How much is it worth? How much income can it produce? Should it make more?

If your business has tangible assets such as land, plant and machinery, or goodwill, it will probably be valued — and that process itself is a high-stakes game because the outcome will significantly impact negotiations and the court outcome.

You'll more than likely have plans for your business but they won't necessarily coincide with other people's ideas for your business. Judges will often look at how profitable your business is, and consider the cash flow, and will then consider whether it could be used to meet housing needs or other claims from your ex-partner and the rest of your family when you get divorced.

You can see how this would be a big problem if you were going to use those cash assets to develop your business in the future.

Protecting Your Business

The best time to read this section is just before you get married... but few of us go into a relationship with the end in sight, so most of us give little thought to what would happen to our business if our relationship ends.

If you want to protect your business before a separation or divorce you need to tread carefully and get specialist advice. If it looks like you're hiding, dissipating, or moving assets or changing shareholdings to avoid future claims in a divorce, your case will be damaged. The court takes a very dim view of such behaviour, and has the power to disregard any actions you take that are specifically designed to avoid future claims.

If your divorce is imminent, it may be too late to take steps to protect your business as much as you'd like, but if you're simply planning for any eventuality, there are a few principles you'll want to keep in mind.

A pre-nuptial or post-nuptial agreement can be helpful in limiting claims against a business. Of course, it may be too late by the time you get to the divorce. If you've strategically planned well ahead at the time you get married or afterwards (for example if you inherit a business) you may be able to get your spouse to agree not to make damaging claims against the business if it all goes wrong in the future.

Do not mix your business assets with your private assets unless absolutely necessary. This is good business advice anyway, but keeping the business entirely separate from your private wealth can help when you divorce. For example, if you use the family home to secure borrowing within the business, that can cause real problems later on.

It is sometimes tempting to involve your partner in the business, not least for tax purposes — and often that will make perfect sense for financial reasons. Keep in mind, though, that involving your partner helps them make a claim because if they've been involved in the business they'll have contributed to its success.

If a business is 100% owned by one person who is getting divorced, the courts will treat it just like any other asset – to be divided or shared, unless there are good reasons not to. If the business is jointly owned with other shareholders or partners the court is less likely to take actions which would damage the livelihoods of the other shareholders or partners.

What's Your Business Worth?

You may have spent years building up your business, so the idea of losing part of it or having it divided in a divorce can be heartbreaking — but it's something you must think about.

You'll need to get your business valued, or agree a value with your ex-partner — and that can be a tricky, specialised job, especially when it comes to the family business. You'll need to consider many factors, including projected income, goodwill, costs of sale, capital gains tax, depreciation costs, and the nature of the business itself.

It's entirely possible your business would be worth very little without your skills and expertise, so it's really important to get a valuation as soon as possible. The sooner you do it, the less likely costs are to escalate and you get a better chance of a fair settlement.

If you and your ex-partner can't agree on the valuation, the court will usually appoint an accountant who'll act on behalf of you both to assess the business.

If you believe the valuation is not accurate based on the evidence you've submitted, you can apply to the court for permission to hire separate accountants to do a valuation. This situation is rare, though, and the court will only agree if the costs are proportionate to your case.

When coming to a settlement, the court will consider the valuation together with all your other family assets. If you have children, the court will decide the best possible outcome for their long-term financial stability and wellbeing. Depending on the valuation and your individual circumstances this may potentially involve selling the business.

In practice, if you have an interest in a family business, the court may decide — or you may reach an agreement — that your ex-partner will take some of the cash or property involved but leave the business itself intact. A business is likely to be an asset that generates income, so any dilution of ownership may affect your future earning potential, which will need to be considered as part of the final settlement.

Things get even more complicated if there are other shareholders involved, so the more comprehensive your initial financial disclosure, the better.

"What should I do first?"

As soon as divorce looks likely, think carefully about what you want to get out of the business, now and in the future. Take good, specialist advice on this from your solicitor, then an accountant. The financial settlement needs to be built around your objectives and needs, and it must be fair to both of you.

If you're a business owner, look at your options for protecting the business (see below). If you're not the business owner, think about the best ways for you to claim a fair share without damaging the continuity of the business. If the business concerned is a farm, there are even more complicated issues and you'll need to look at the specific problems facing farms during divorce.

A Family Business

If possible, the courts try to leave the business owner with the business and compensate the other partner with a larger share of the other assets and/or maintenance. Very often, this is what the couple wants, too — especially the person owning and running the business.

The problem with this approach is it's difficult to put an accurate value on a business, so it's hard to know whether or not it's fair. Added to that is the difficulty in forecasting how well the business will do in the future.

Courts can be flexible — it is possible to share the income or divide shares. In an ideal world, they prefer not to put all the illiquid assets with one partner and the liquid assets with the other — but in reality, this can happen.

You'll want to be clear about what approach you want to take, because every business is different. Start by considering the following points:

- What income does the business produce?

- Does the business support a high standard of living — maybe more in real terms than just the income or dividend stream?

- Does the business contain property or assets, and are they valuable?

- Is there a company or business pension? If so, what value does that have, either in savings, property or shares?

- Is it possible to pull cash from the business to provide money for housing?

- Is it possible to borrow against the business or its assets?

- Is the ownership of the business shared? If so, is this with family members who would act together by agreement or with people outside the family whose interests are different?

Not all businesses have to be valued — some, like partnerships, are simply income streams. If there's nothing to sell, only the income stream matters and that doesn't need to be valued because you can share it via a maintenance order.

If one spouse owns a business outright, or has a significant shareholding, usually the business will need to be valued.

If the business *is* owned outright by you or your ex-partner — or jointly by both of you — the court is more likely to treat it as just another family asset to be divided appropriately.

If it's owned by several people, and you or your spouse has a minority shareholding, the value of the shareholding is relevant to your divorce. In this case, the court is less likely to ask for business assets to be sold, or to pull cash out of the business in other ways. To do so would damage the interests of people outside the marriage and that's not fair to them.

"Will I have to sell the business?"

The courts can order businesses to be sold, but it's very unusual. It's much more likely the court will allocate the non-business owner to have more of the property or cash outside the business or order maintenance to be paid out of the business's income stream.

Your best option is to sit down at the start and discuss this with your ex-partner, and with your solicitors. Fighting about it in court is extremely expensive and time-consuming, not to mention incredibly stressful.

Whether you're the business owner or not, it's vital to take independent legal advice from your specialist family solicitor as soon as possible.

Most importantly, if you're the business owner — don't panic and make changes to the business. This can damage your position because such changes are obviously designed to make negotiations difficult. That doesn't mean you can't take sensible steps to reduce your risk —

just don't do anything in a panic, and don't do anything without professional advice.

If you're not the business owner, you'll want to make sure the business isn't being jeopardised — either because it has borrowings that are too large, or because your ex-partner is making changes to cut you out. It is possible to ask a court to disregard changes which are designed to limit your claims — so you must move quickly and take expert legal advice if you think this is happening.

"Should I fight the claims?"

Our first piece of advice to you, as a business owner, is keep cool and calm and sit down with your solicitor right at the start to think things over. You need to understand what might happen if you go to court — how the whole process works and what it costs.

Think about what you're prepared to offer or negotiate to prevent things ever getting as far as court:

- Are you willing to share the income from the business?

- Are you prepared to share the ownership of the business — now, or in future?

- If you're planning to sell your business when you retire, would you be willing to share part of the proceeds at that point?

- What do you plan to do about retirement?

- Do you have any plans to pass the business onto your children?

You must be prepared, because if you don't set the agenda for your discussions with your ex-partner, the whole thing will be out of your control.

So, make an appointment to see a specialist family solicitor as far in advance of your divorce as possible.

Think about what you want to achieve with your business, and talk about your worries about what might happen when you get divorced.

If your divorce is imminent, arrange a meeting fast. But even if you're only thinking about separation right now, you'll be wise to start preparing for the worst because your solicitor will be able to advise you what you can do to protect your business, and what you absolutely should not do.

Losing your business is not inevitable; a lot will depend on the nature of your business, and how amicable you and your ex-partner can be. A good, experienced family solicitor will be able to help you get the best outcome for you and your family.

Summary

- You'll need to prepare a financial disclosure for your business in the same way you do for your personal wealth and assets — and you'll need to be scrupulously honest.

- Tread carefully if you want to take steps to protect your business. Any actions you take that are obviously designed to limit your ex-partner's claims will be disregarded by the court and will damage your own case.

- Get in touch with an experienced family solicitor as soon as you suspect your relationship may be in trouble — and immediately if your divorce is imminent. The more you know and understand, the better prepared you'll be, and the better the outcome for you and your family.

If you have children, Chapter 6 is going to be one of the most helpful pieces of information for you. The next chapter will help you navigate what is probably the most emotionally fraught part of divorce — and the more you understand, the better the outcome for your children (and you).

Notes

Chapter 6

Think of the Children

How to make arrangements that are best for everyone

Probably the most emotive area of family law and the separation and divorce process concerns children.

If you're a parent considering or going through a divorce, you're probably worried about how your children will cope.

We always find emotions run high when we're helping parents organise and — hopefully — agree to arrangements about where children should live, and what time they should spend with the parent they don't live with.

Ultimately, the primary focus is on the children's welfare and what is in their best interests. The courts see children's welfare as their most important consideration — and this is the overriding objective throughout the whole process.

This often causes tension between parents, especially when they're at odds — but you must remember to keep children out of any disputes.

When you're considering the arrangements for your children, by far the best course of action is to reach an agreement between you and your ex-partner. If you're unable to do this, you might want to bring in a solicitor to help you reach an agreement. If you still can't reach an agreement, you should turn to Alternative Dispute Resolution (ADR).

We want you to be prepared to deal with some of the sensitive challenges you're likely to face over the coming weeks and months, so in this chapter you'll be able to find everything you need to know about your legal rights, as well as practical suggestions to help you and your children manage during what can be a very traumatic time for families.

Before we go into all that, though, we want to get rid of any confusion around legal terminology and children's arrangements, because it has changed over the years.

You may have heard the terms "custody" and "access" and "residence", "residency" and "contact" but we no longer use such terms. After the Children and Families Act 2014 came into force in April 2014, arrangements for children are now defined using the terms "living with" and "spending time with"... which is much simpler for everyone to understand.

This chapter is all about walking you through everything you need to know about the law and children when it comes to divorce — so let's start at the beginning.

Parental Responsibility

Parental responsibility is defined in section 3(1) of the Children Act 1989 as "all the rights, duties, powers, responsibilities and authority which by law a parent of a child has in relation to the child and his property."

That's the legal jargon. What it actually means is "parental responsibility" gives parents the right to make all the important decisions in a child's life — such as which school they attend, or what religion they'll follow (if any).

It sounds fairly straightforward — after all, if you're a child's parent, you automatically have responsibility for them, don't you?

Well, yes if you're the mother. But if you're the father, and you weren't married to the child's mother when it was born, it's not quite that simple.

All mothers automatically have parental responsibility for the child from birth, unless they surrender that responsibility through adoption.

For fathers, it depends on your circumstances. If you were married when your child was born, you'll have parental responsibility as the child's father.

If you were unmarried when your child was born, the child's date of birth matters. If your child was born after December 1, 2003 and you were named on the birth certificate, you'll have parental responsibility. If your child was born before that date, only the mother will automatically have parental responsibility.

If you don't have parental responsibility, you can obtain it by doing one of the following:

- If you married the mother of your child after its birth, you'll have gained parental responsibility.

- You can apply to the court for a parental responsibility order.

- You can make a parental responsibility agreement (in a set procedure) with the child's mother.

- You can apply for — and get — a residence order.

- You can be appointed the child's guardian.

Parental responsibility can only be terminated by adoption or a court order. With a court order, the parent needs to get permission from the court and the child, as long as the child can understand what's going on. It doesn't happen often, and the court doesn't take it lightly — but it can be justified in certain circumstances.

In one case that went to the Court of Appeal, a father's parental responsibility was terminated after he had gone to prison for sexually abusing his own child's half-sisters. The court decided the child's emotional and psychological security would be in jeopardy if the father continued to remain in the child's life.

You should note that a parental responsibility order doesn't automatically give the non-residence parent any rights to have contact with the child — you'll still need to work those arrangements out with your ex-partner.

Making Contact Arrangements

The court will always work on a "no order principle" where they can — they much prefer families to work out issues relating to children by mutual agreement rather than having to go to court.

Our experience of working with families shows this is by far the best way to go about things, for the children and for you.

But we also know that, even with the best of intentions on all sides, it's not always possible for parents to reach an agreement without outside help.

Your first port of call should be one of the Alternative Dispute Resolution (ADR) methods detailed in Chapter 2 — and you should talk to your family solicitor for advice and guidance, too.

Applying to the Court

If you're unable to reach an agreement with your ex-partner directly, through solicitors or through ADR, you may have to apply to the court under Section 8 of the

Children Act 1989. The court can make the following orders:

Child Arrangement Order

This used to be called a contact and residence order, but it was renamed in 2014. The old-style contact and residence orders made some parents feel like they were either a winner or a loser.

The aim of the order is to send a clear message to parents that both of you will be bringing up your children together.

The order defines who the children live with and who they spend time with. If you agree a shared care arrangement with your ex-partner, the child arrangement order can state that your children live with both parents — but that doesn't necessarily mean they'll spend half their time with you and half with your ex-partner, because this could be very disruptive.

Prohibited Steps Order

A prohibited steps order prevents one parent from doing something specific. A parent might apply for this order to prevent the other parent taking the child out of the country. If one parent is worried the other parent may not bring the child back, this order may be granted — especially if the country in question isn't a member of the Hague Convention.

Specific Issue Order

This order enables the court to decide on a specific issue relating to a child, particularly in emergency situations. It can only be made to enable a parent to meet their parental responsibility.

Here are some examples of specific issue orders (these are only examples, and there are many more possibilities):

- One parent doesn't want their child to have medical treatment.
- For the child to attend a specific school.
- Deciding on the child's surname.

The court will only grant a specific issue order if it considers it absolutely necessary — and will always put the child's welfare first. A child arrangements order is often made at the same time as a specific issue order.

Who Can Apply for a Court Order?

If you want to apply for a court order under Section 8 of the Children Act 1989, you might find you need the court's permission to do so.

If you're one of the following, you don't need permission and you can go ahead and apply for a court order:

1. The parent, guardian or special guardian of a child
2. Anyone with parental responsibility
3. Anyone with a child residence order

4.   Anyone in a marriage or civil partnership where the child is a child of the family

5.   Anyone with whom the child has lived for at least three years

6.   Anyone who has permission from:

- A residence order

- The local authority if the child is in their care

- Everyone who has parental responsibility for the child

Other people can ask the Court for permission to give an application for a child arrangements order. Before the court decides whether or not to grant permission, though, it will consider:

- The nature of the application

- The applicant's connection with the child

- Any risk of disruption to the child's life to such an extent it would harm them

It's becoming more and more common for grandparents to apply to the court — and to do so, they must get permission from the court first.

Before the court makes any order, though, it will carefully consider the Welfare Checklist.

The Welfare Checklist

The court will consider seven key factors when making any decisions about children. This is the "welfare checklist" and is included in section 1(3) of the Children Act 1989.

An officer from The Children and Family Court Advisory and Support Service (CAFCASS) will put together a welfare report and take into account:

1. The child's wishes and feelings

2. The child's physical, emotional and educational needs

3. How a change in circumstances following the court's decision might affect the child

4. The child's age, sex, background and any other characteristics which will be relevant to the court's decision

5. Any harm the child has suffered or may be at risk of suffering

6. How capable the child's parents (or any other relevant people) are at meeting the child's needs

7. The powers available to the Court in any particular case

The child's wishes & feelings

Depending on how old the child is, and whether they can understand their circumstances, the court will consider the child's wishes and feelings.

There's no fixed age at which the court will consult children, because maturity and understanding are different for every child.

When making a decision, the court will also look at whether or not a child's wishes and feelings are their own, or if they may have been influenced by someone else.

The CAFCASS worker will meet with the child to find out if there's any influence, and will include that in their report to the court.

The child's physical, emotional, and educational needs

Contrary to popular mythology, there's no assumption or presumption that children will automatically stay with their mother. She will still have to demonstrate she can meet the child's day-to-day needs.

The court's job is to look at who's in the best position to meet the child's emotional, physical and education needs. It tries hard to keep things as they are to make sure the child's life is disrupted as little as possible. As always, the child's welfare is the primary consideration.

The effect of a change of circumstances

The court wants to make sure any change in the child's circumstances will have as little effect on them as possible — and that the change will be for the child's benefit.

Child's age, sex, background, and other characteristics

The court may consider issues like religion and culture when it's making a decision — as well as the parents' lifestyle, or any new partners, if any of these factors are likely to affect the child negatively.

Any harm the child could suffer

The courts will consider any harm the child has suffered in the past — as well as any harm they're likely to suffer. The idea is to minimise any distress to the child.

Harm can be emotional, physical, sexual, psychological, or financial.

Parents' capability to meet child's needs

Each parent must demonstrate they're capable and committed to meeting the child's daily needs. The court must be satisfied the child is living with the parent best-suited to look after them, or that both parents are able to care for the child.

Range of powers available to the court

When making its decision, the court has to consider *all* the orders available to it — the child arrangements order, the prohibited steps order, the specific issue order, and others like the special guardianship order.

How to Apply for a Court Order

Before you can make an application to court, both you and your ex-partner must attend a MIAM meeting to encourage an amicable agreement — and to filter out any cases that should never go to court at all.

There are some instances in which you wouldn't have to attend MIAM, which include:

- Allegations of domestic violence
- Urgency
- No mediator within 15 miles of the applicant's home
- Where social services are involved because of child welfare concerns
- Disabilities preventing someone from accessing a mediator
- Where you don't want to notify your ex-partner

When you've applied and paid the correct court fee, the court will list your case for a hearing — the First Hearing Dispute Resolution Appointment (FHDRA).

You'll normally wait a few months before a judge hears your case, so you'll both need a lot of patience. This is just one reason why applying to court should be a last resort for most people.

At the FHDRA, the judge will listen to the issues and reasons for your application. A Children and Family Court Advisory and Support Service (CAFCASS) officer will attend the hearing — and they are not there to persuade the judge but help the judge make a decision. The judge may order the CAFCASS officer to put together a report on the impact of the application on the welfare of the child. And if the child is old enough, the judge may ask the CAFCASS officer to prepare a report about the child's wishes and feelings.

At the hearing, the judge will outline what steps need to be taken — for example, a CAFCASS report, police disclosure, or witness statements, if necessary.

Your case will then be listed for another hearing.

There is no hard and fast rule as to how many hearings are necessary. If anyone has made allegations which can have serious consequences for the child, the judge will usually order everyone to complete a schedule of allegations and list the matter for a fact-finding hearing, which may last a few days.

The whole process of going to court is very stressful and costly, and there's little anyone can do to eliminate that. But it's made worse by having to wait for a court date. Despite the introduction of MIAMS, the courts have fallen victim to government cuts — which only cause further delays. It's fairly common for cases to run more than a year before they can be resolved.

Family break-ups are almost always distressing. Even more so if children are involved.

However, it is possible to work things out amicably and we strongly advise you to do so if you can possibly manage it. It's best for your children, best for you, and best for the rest of your family.

If you have no choice but to go to court, you'll need to be patient: the process may be lengthy, expensive, and stressful — but focus on the end goal and always, always think about your children because whatever decisions you make now will continue to have an effect on them as they grow up.

Client Stories

As you can imagine, many of our clients are worried about what will happen to the children — and whether or not they'll be able to have as much contact with them as they'd like. We're sharing these stories so you know you're not alone, and you can get the best possible outcome for your whole family.

Our client came in for an initial consultation because his wife had stopped him from seeing his children. He was understandably devastated as he absolutely dotes on his children, and had previously instructed another law firm but was unhappy with the service.

We advised him to make an application to court. He was reluctant at first because he knew he'd have to wait at least six weeks for a hearing date, which meant more time away from his children. But his wife refused to enter into any negotiations.

We kept in regular contact with the client and spoke to him often when he was feeling down about not seeing his children. We attended a FHDRA to deal with the issue and managed to arrange for him to see his children for an hour the next day. He was overjoyed and called to tell us how well the contact had gone and how she loved seeing her father.

We were able to arrange supervised contact for a few sessions up to the final hearing. Luckily for our client, we were able to avoid that final hearing and we reached an agreement between solicitors that works really well for him. He now has regular contact with his children, they stay with him on alternate weekends, for one evening in the week, and talk on the telephone often. He and his ex have also agreed contact for the school holidays.

Whenever we speak to him he always thanks us, because he knows he couldn't have done this alone.

Another client was in a bitter dispute with his ex-partner over their child. The mother moved out of the family home shortly after the child was born and our client travelled to see his child every fortnight without fail at his parents' home.

This went on for three years until the mother stopped all contact without telling our client why. He applied for a child arrangement order — which is when the mother raised allegations of sexual abuse while the child was in his care. Police and social services investigated, as you would expect.

Social services interviewed the child — but at the fact-finding hearing carried out under the child arrangement application, the social worker was heavily criticised for asking leading questions and interviewing a young child for over an hour without a break or any refreshments. The judge found the interviews wholly unreliable and found they did not comply with guidelines. The child was only under five at the time.

After a four-day fact-finding hearing, the judge found in favour of the mother despite the unreliable evidence. We were all astounded, including the mother. In fact, we'd been in discussions with the mother about arranging contact before the judgement was handed down. Our client had already been interviewed by the police and the judgement would have resulted in him being charged, potentially imprisoned and put on the Sex Offenders Register. Our client felt he had no choice but to appeal the decision to clear his name, save his reputation, and repair the damage caused to his relationship with his child.

At the appeal hearing the judge found the trial judge didn't consider the allegations within the context they were made and that he had made a mistake in relying completely on the mother's evidence. He also found the original judge made a mistake by not providing substantive reasons why our client was not a credible witness. The judge felt the child had been unnecessarily pushed by the mother and failed by social services.

The findings against our client, the father, were set aside. The allegations against him were not proved and the case went forward on the basis the abuse never happened. This was a big result for everyone involved.

Our client was granted supervised contact at a contact centre with his child until the final hearing. The judge was very keen to conclude everything quickly because he felt the child had been denied the opportunity to have a relationship with the father. Our client saw his child for the first time in many months and although the child was shy at first, the contact reports state they hugged and kissed at the end of the first session. This did not stop the mother from alleging the child was distressed after contact, which was proven to be false.

At the final hearing the judge ordered that the child was to see the father unsupervised every fortnight with overnight stays, shared holidays and mid-week contact. Result! We could not have asked for anything more.

We saw another father who was extremely distressed because he'd been prevented from seeing his two young children. He'd been in a very volatile relationship with the children's mother, who later accused him of stalking and harassing her, when in reality he was simply desperate to see his children.

He sent the mother a letter, pleading with her to allow him to see the children, but he sent the letter after the police had officially warned him not to contact his ex-partner. As a result, he was charged and found guilty of harassment.

Our client was at an extremely low ebb, but after we started proceedings under the Children Act for a Child Arrangements Order, we were secured supervised contact in a contact centre. This continued for several months, and although the mother sometimes failed to co-operate, our client did form an excellent relationship with his children, who began to get used to him again, and really looked forward to seeing him. He was absolutely thrilled when his youngest child called him "Daddy" for the first time!

Our client didn't have much hope of ever seeing his children on his own, because of how his ex-partner had behaved throughout. At the final hearing, he was worried the court would be taken in by all her "woes" — but this wasn't the case. The contact centre staff and the social worker could see how dedicated our client was to his children. It was all documented in the contact notes and the social services report, which the court received.

In the end, the court ordered that our client should see his children more and more often away from the centre. His visits increased from a few hours to a day, then overnight at the weekends. The court also ordered Christmas and birthday visits, because there was no doubt that having their father in their lives was most certainly in the best interests of these two children.

Had the father not got legal advice, bearing in mind his ex-partner's level of hostility, it's extremely unlikely that he would have been able to see his children regularly. Having taken court action, he is now an active part of his children's lives. He can watch them grow, and he plays an important role in their development, in a way that every diligent father should be able to do."

Summary

- Mothers automatically have parental responsibility — and so do fathers if they were married when the child was born. If you don't have parental responsibility, there are a number of ways you can get it.

- The orders the court can make when it comes to children are: child arrangement orders, prohibited steps orders, and specific issues orders.

- Grandparents are increasingly applying to the courts for orders, but they need to get permission to do so.

- If you can work things out amicably, either by discussing things together or by using alternative dispute resolution methods, that's by far the best way for everyone — going to court can take more than a year.

- Even if you've been prevented from contacting your children, don't give up hope. But you must get good legal advice — trying to go it alone is a recipe for disaster.

In the next chapter, we'll be looking at how domestic violence affects divorce proceedings, and what help is available if this affects you.

Notes

Chapter 7

How to Cope with an Abusive Partner

You're not alone — and you can get help

You may be surprised to learn that "domestic violence" isn't just physical violence. In fact, most forms of domestic abuse aren't physical at all… yet.

And it doesn't just affect women and children, although they make up the vast majority of victims. Men can be victims of domestic abuse too. Throughout this chapter we're using the term "domestic abuse" to include all forms of abuse, both physical and emotional.

Many people consider "domestic violence" to be actual physical violence against a person — or an imminent threat of physical violence. As a result many people remain in unhappy relationships where they tolerate unacceptable behaviour.

They become more and more isolated from family and friends, while their partner criticises and belittles them, because they feel there's nothing they can do about it.

This isn't true — domestic abuse exists in many ways within a marriage or relationship and you don't have to tolerate it. Nobody should find themselves in a relationship where their partner behaves unreasonably towards them. Over time, they may begin to feel worthless, lose their confidence, and slowly become a "victim" in their relationship rather than a partner.

Ultimately, this cycle usually leads to depression, emotional turmoil, insecurity, and isolation or loneliness. And if the behaviour carries on long enough and is extreme enough, it can end in death or serious injury.

We've all heard stories on the news about people who suffered for years, and whose lives ended in tragedy. We often wonder how this could happen; why they didn't leave. The reasons are many and complicated, but it's important to realise that in most cases, they didn't go into an abusive relationship; they went into a relationship that became abusive over time, so slowly and insidiously that it was almost impossible to notice it.

When this type of behaviour happens often and over a long period of time, the victim slowly begins to accept that this type of behaviour is acceptable and normal — because it doesn't happen all at once.

Victims of domestic abuse often feel embarrassed and humiliated by their treatment and are too frightened to ask for help. Unfortunately, this is very common. But you're not alone — unfortunately domestic violence and abuse affect one in four women and one in six men during their lifetime, regardless of age, race, disability or lifestyle.

The UK has a "zero tolerance" attitude towards domestic abuse and the courts take abusive behaviour very seriously. If your children are also subjected to abusive behaviour from your partner, or are witnessing abuse within their home, the courts will make orders to protect them from the perpetrator — sometimes even severing all contact between the perpetrator and the children.

The Government defines domestic abuse as *"any incident or pattern of incidents of controlling, coercive, threatening, violence or abuse between those aged 16 or over who are, or have been, intimate partners or family members regardless of gender or sexuality."*

Such abuse can involve, but is not limited to:

- Psychological
- Physical
- Sexual
- Financial

- Emotional

Domestic abuse also includes "honour based violence", forced marriage, female genital mutilation (FMG), and stalking.

It's really important to understand that most domestic abuse doesn't start as physical violence — but much of it ends there. Looking at past cases of domestic abuse, we know strangulation is one of the most potentially lethal forms. A study conducted in 2001 found 10% of violent deaths in the United States were attributable to strangulation and most victims were women.

The UK and the United States are similar enough in culture for this study to be relevant to domestic abuse in this country.

It's Not Your Fault

Where women are the victims of domestic abuse, and women are the most likely to suffer in this way, some societies perceive it's the woman's fault.

This perception is changing, slowly, but the belief is so ingrained in some societies that many women believe it as well as men.

Add to this the fact there are some cultures where women are still not able to choose whom they marry and whether or not to stay in a relationship, and you can see how many people find it so difficult to leave abusive relationships.

Most of us look back, on occasion, to times when we wish we'd done something differently. Victims of violence and abuse often do the same thing — but if this is you, you must not blame yourself. If someone tries to control you by saying cruel things, making threats, or acting dangerously towards you *it is not your fault*. It is their fault.

An abusive partner's destructive behaviour is *not* your responsibility. It's theirs, and there is no excuse for it. Abuse is not caused by alcohol, drugs, poverty, or any other external factor (although they can certainly make things worse). Abuse is all about power, and abusers want power over their victims.

Until the victim takes action or the aggressor accepts they have a problem and asks for help, the victim will continue to be a victim. Difficult though it is — and sometimes it seems impossible — you can take action against destructive behaviour and you can start living a fulfilled and happy life.

If you believe you're suffering at the hands of your partner who's subjecting you to ongoing abusive or unreasonable behaviour — or they're physically violent towards you — you do not need to tolerate it and there are ways to deal with it.

"What are my options?"

By far the most difficult step of all is the first one: making the decision to get help then actually doing it.

The first thing many people want to do is talk to someone — and we'd like to assure you there is always someone you can talk to, even if you feel you can't talk to friends or family.

There are a number of domestic abuse charities across the UK, such as Dash — Domestic Abuse Stops Here. You can find them at www.thedashcharity.org.uk or call their helpline on 01753 549865.

You can also contact Women's Aid via their website: www.womensaid.org.uk.

Or Refuge: www.refuge.org.uk

Their shared helpline is 0808 2000 247 and it's open 24 hours.

Their services are free and confidential, and they can give you support and advise you on your options.

When you feel able to take the next step in finding freedom from domestic abuse, they will assess and complete a support plan tailored to your individual family needs. They'll support you throughout, both emotionally and with safety planning and crisis intervention, including safe housing accommodation. They're also trained to support and help your children.

"How does domestic abuse affect my children?"

Unfortunately, it's well known that children and young people who suffer or witness domestic abuse are three times more likely to suffer emotional difficulties including low self-esteem, aggressive behaviour, and other behavioural difficulties which could affect their own future relationships.

It's really important you seek help from trained professionals so your children have the best chance of coming through their experiences healthy.

"What if my partner won't accept my decision?"

The aggressor in an abusive relationship often feels like they "own" their partner — so it's very common for an abusive partner to feel like they've lost control and ownership when someone takes steps to stop domestic abuse. The abusive partner may resort to threatening, harassing, and intimidating behaviour to prevent their partner leaving, and to try to regain control.

This is a critical time, because it's at this stage many people return to abusive relationships for fear of the consequences if they don't. If you're in this position, you'll need all your strength and as much support as you can find from professionals and friends and family, to leave the abuse behind and find freedom.

If you find your ex-partner tries to prevent you leaving, you can ask the court to take steps to protect you and your children, so you can move on and begin your new life.

The Court's Role

The Family Law Act 1996 gives the court the power to make a variety of orders, including a non-molestation order forbidding an abusive partner from using or threatening violence against you. It also prevents them from harassing, pestering, or intimidating you.

The court can also order that there's no communication between you — including preventing other people like your ex-partner's family and friends from acting on their instructions.

If there are any children, the court can also prevent an abusive partner from contacting them.

"Why should I leave my home if I'm the victim?"

No victim of domestic abuse should feel they have to leave their home, their friends, or their family because of someone else's behaviour. So as well as a non-molestation order, the court can sometimes make an occupation order.

In this case, the abusive partner must leave the family home and isn't allowed to return for a specified period of time. That way, the victim of the abuse and any children can stay in their home.

If the situation is urgent, you may be able to get a short-term non-molestation order immediately and without notifying your abusive ex-partner. In extreme and rare cases, you may be able to get an occupation order at the same time.

These orders can stay in force for up to a year and can be extended if necessary. They also carry a power of arrest, which allows the police to arrest someone if they break the order.

The Power of Arrest

Once you've got an order from the court, a process server must serve it personally on your ex-partner. When that has happened, you're entitled to call the police if you believe your ex-partner has broken the order. The police will arrest the person, and they'll have to go before the court as soon as possible.

The power of arrest is particularly effective over weekends or bank holidays when you may have less support than during the working week.

The police can hold the perpetrator until they're able to take them to court.

If the court finds your ex-partner has breached the order, they'll be punished — which could include an immediate prison sentence, a suspended prison sentence, a fine, or community service. The punishment will depend on how serious the breach was.

"Can I get Legal Aid?"

At the time of writing this book, it currently doesn't cost anything to apply to the family court for a domestic violence injunction. In some circumstances, you may be able to get public funding for legal help to get any of the orders we've mentioned. The Legal Aid Agency will be able to assess you and find out if this is possible.

If you're not eligible for Legal Aid, you can find a solicitor privately, or if you feel able you can apply to the court yourself. However, if you've been manipulated and bullied, and you're afraid of your ex-partner, this may not be a good idea. The more help and support you can get, the better.

Most importantly of all, if you are or have been a victim of domestic abuse, please remember you're not alone and *it's not your fault*. And remember, too, that you don't have to suffer anymore — there is a way out when you're ready to take it and there is help available.

Client Stories

We worked with a client who was desperately trying to escape an abusive marriage. This is her story...

Our client was anxious. Couldn't stop crying and couldn't focus on any of the questions we were asking her.

And no wonder, because she'd been in an abusive relationship for years. Her husband had physically and mentally abused her, systematically destroying her confidence and her self-esteem. She felt worthless. She'd been *made* to feel worthless.

Her husband would hit her, then put his hand over her mouth to stop her from crying. He'd make her eat food from the floor if he was angry. She spent her marriage living in fear of upsetting him because he'd become angry for days on end...and she'd never know what the punishment would be.

She knew she wanted to get divorced — she couldn't stay in an abusive marriage any longer. But she was afraid of what would happen when her husband found out, so we made an emergency application to court for a non-molestation order. It was successful and gave our client the protection she needed to move forward with her divorce.

We've kept in touch with her throughout — then we saw her two months later at court for the return hearing of the non-molestation proceedings, and she looked and seemed like a different person. She was stronger, she was able to smile, and she said she just felt happy knowing he could no longer threaten her.

She has her good days and her bad days, as is normal with the breakdown of a marriage — but she said the most important thing she has now is peace of mind, knowing her husband can no longer dominate, control and punish her.

Another client came to us after 30 years of marriage, proving it's never too late to make a positive change...

Our client was retired. She'd been married to her husband for many years, suffering significantly because of ongoing domestic violence. Her husband would regularly strangle her, throw her downstairs, threaten her with a knife — and much more. There was much medical evidence to support past injuries.

But she'd simply been too afraid to do anything about it. When she contacted the police, her husband threatened her with financial hardship if she pushed it further. Finally, she contacted us after her husband assaulted her again. She'd contacted DASH in desperation, and they referred her to us. This time, a relative supported her and convinced her to report it to the police. Her husband was arrested, charged with assault, and bailed.

We met here on the same day she contacted us. We were shocked at how this lady's suffering, for such a long period of time, had affected her. She would visibly jump if there was a loud noise. She was constantly looking around her and she was extremely nervous and anxious. She'd grown so nervous she couldn't drive her car anymore. Her husband had made her feel that she was worthless and a waste of space, and we were horrified to see an elderly lady in such a state.

With our support and her relative's support, we got an ex parte order against her husband the next day, giving her a non-molestation order and occupation order so she could live in her home. He was forbidden from returning to the family home for 12 months and was not allowed to use or threaten any violence against her for the same period. At the return hearing, she was so frightened we got the judge's permission for her not to come into court.

One of the reasons she'd never had the strength to escape was money: her husband had threatened repeatedly to leave her poor. We asked the court, under the Family Law Act, for another occupation order ordering her husband to contribute financially to the family home for 12 months. This allowed our client to rest peacefully at home away from her violent and abusive husband and without worrying about paying the bills. She could begin to recover and start her new life.

Since then she's grown strong enough to start divorce proceedings and, after some difficult negotiating between us and the husband's solicitor, a financial settlement was eventually reached, allowing her to stay in her home.

Her life has taken a dramatic change for the better since we first met her. She now drives and goes to the gym regularly. Although she'll always be a little nervous, she's improved enormously since we first met. And she often tells us she considers us as friends and will be forever grateful for what we've helped her do.

Taking all this action has given our client enough courage to stand up to her abuser in court — and her husband was found guilty of all charges. It's never too late to change your life.

Summary

- Domestic violence and domestic abuse aren't just physical abuse — it can involve (but is not limited to) psychological, sexual, financial, physical, and emotional abuse.

- It's not your fault! You are not responsible for someone else's abusive and destructive behaviour. Abuse is all about power; it's not caused by alcohol, drugs, poverty, or any other external factor (although they can make things worse).

- You can ask for help from local Berkshire charity Dash (Domestic Abuse Stops Here) or national charities Women's Aid and Refuge.

- Men can suffer domestic abuse too — and although most victims are women, men should feel they can ask for help too.

- The court has the power to intervene to protect you and your children if necessary — by ensuring you can stay in your home, and by cutting contact with your ex-partner.

The Family Team at Parfitt Cresswell offer specialist advice and help for people suffering from domestic violence and abuse. We understand how difficult it can be to ask for help — but if you're ready to talk to a solicitor, or you'd simply like to visit us to talk about your situation, we'd like to invite you to a free, completely confidential face-to-face meeting (valued at £200) with one of our expert family lawyers. You can come to any of our offices, and make sure you find a solicitor who understands your individual needs and will look after your best interests.

Simply call 0800 015 2843, or you can email us at tgdg@parfittcresswell.com and book a time to come and tell us about your relationship.

Notes

Chapter 8

Getting Married

"Do I need a prenuptial agreement?"

We've talked a lot about divorce, but let's look at another big event in your life: getting married. If you're going through a divorce at the moment, getting married again may be the last thing you want to think about — but planning ahead is a good idea.

We're often asked, "Do I need a prenuptial agreement?" and the answer is always the same: although it doesn't seem very romantic, we would strongly advise you to organise one.

Nobody goes into a relationship planning to get divorced, but if the worst happens and you have a prenuptial agreement, it can save a lot of stress and unhappiness at an already stressful and unhappy time, if your marriage does end.

Although courts in England and Wales still don't treat prenuptial agreements as 100% binding, and they take serious changes in circumstances into account (like having children), they are far more likely to uphold the original agreement you make.

Why Get A Prenuptial Agreement?

Apart from allowing you both to go into a marriage with your eyes wide open, another advantage of a prenup is it can help to keep your divorce out of the courts if you split up later on.

If you do go to court, accredited members of the press can sit in on and report on divorce cases. If one or both of you is in the public eye, or is significantly wealthy, there'll always be some media interest. A prenup will help you keep your divorce and finances private.

If you're marrying late in life and one or both of you brings significant assets to the marriage, a prenup is particularly important. In cases like this, it may be that one of you brings more to the marriage than the other, or one of you will stand to benefit from an inheritance because of the marriage. It's perfectly reasonable to protect your own position as an individual, especially if you have assets you want to protect for your children and prevent them being lost to a claim by your ex-partner on divorce.

They can also be useful for professional athletes, or others who are capable of earning a lot of money for a relatively short period in their careers. A prenup can help them protect the assets they built up before getting married, to provide them with financial security once their high-earning career has ended.

Creating a Prenup

If you do decide to have a prenuptial agreement, it must be fair and balanced. If one partner can show the other had an unfair advantage when the agreement was written, the court may disregard it altogether — or rely on it less during the divorce.

When you sit down and put it together, you should both start by disclosing all your assets, including properties, savings, and any accounts you both have — shared or individual. You should both get independent legal advice from separate solicitors to make sure you both understand the agreement you're entering into.

If you go into the agreement in this manner, you'll both know exactly what you're signing and why, so there's no confusion and no opportunity for anyone to claim they were misled later on.

We recommend you allow as much time as possible to sort your prenup out. The Law Commission suggests you should enter into any agreement at least 28 days before your wedding to avoid any suggestion it may have been signed "under duress" — so start talking about it in plenty of time.

This may not be easy, because it's not exactly the most romantic way to enter a marriage... although the most successful marriages are ones in which both partners are practical and clear-headed about their life together.

You should bear in mind if you move abroad, your English prenuptial agreement may not be valid. There is no such thing as a globally recognised prenup at the moment. If you do move abroad after getting married, you should take legal advice in the country you move to.

Likewise, if you have moved to England or Wales from abroad you should get legal advice from a solicitor here as to whether or not any agreements you have are valid in this country.

If you do get a prenup, you should consider updating it every few years — and particularly if you have a major change of circumstances, like having children, suffering a disability or serious illness, or inheriting money or property. An updated prenuptial agreement is known as a post-nuptial — and it will help to keep things clear in case of divorce in the future.

Summary

- A prenuptial agreement isn't 100% legally binding, but courts generally uphold it — however they do take into account a change in circumstances, like having children.

- Prenups are particularly important if you're marrying late in life, or if one of you is particularly wealthy.

- Having a prenup can help to keep any future divorce and financial affairs private, because it can help to keep you out of court.

Whatever stage you're at in your relationship, next steps are important. One of the most useful and important things you can do early on is find a solicitor you trust. In the next section, we'll explain what to look for in a family law solicitor, and how to make sure you work with the right person.

Notes

Next Steps

What does your future hold?

At this point, we hope you have a much better understanding of divorce and marriage law in England and Wales, whether you're going into a new relationship or facing the end of one.

The beginning or end of a relationship is a huge event in anyone's life, which is why it's so important you get all the support you need.

Friends, family, and professional counsellors should be your first stop for emotional support — but an experienced, compassionate family law solicitor should be your first port of call for legal advice. So, with all this information at your fingertips, why is it such a good idea to see an experienced family lawyer... and what should you look for?

The most important characteristic you should look for in a family solicitor is experience. The wider the variety of divorces and separations they've dealt with, the better they'll know exactly what's needed to resolve your divorce in the way you hope. Some solicitors just do occasional family law work alongside other areas of law, such as wills, and probate, and property sales, and purchase. This isn't ideal because they won't have the day-to-day experience and knowledge of the way the courts are interpreting family legislation.

At Parfitt Cresswell, our family law team are all full-time family lawyers with many years of experience, which means they're best placed to ensure you achieve the very best outcome in your circumstances.

You'll recall we mentioned back in Chapter 4 that the courts have a wide discretion under the section 25 considerations of the Matrimonial Causes Act. There can be a substantial difference between one end of discretion and the other... and a good solicitor will make sure you're on the right side of this discretion.

Ideally, your solicitor will be a member of Resolution, which means they'll be committed to dealing with your divorce in as amicable a way as possible. A good solicitor will not want you to go to court, and they'll do their absolute best to keep you on good terms with your ex-partner so you can avoid court.

They'll be able to advise you on alternative dispute resolution methods, like mediation or collaborative law — and help you decide on the best course for you and your family.

But experience and legal knowledge, while essential, are not enough on their own. A truly exceptional family solicitor will combine their skills with empathy and compassion, helping you keep your emotions under control and resolving your situation without escalating it to the courts.

This means they'll be willing to tell you some hard truths when necessary — so when you're looking for the right solicitor for your case, choose someone who'll advise on what's best for you, even if you don't like hearing it at the time. A great solicitor will be able to do that with compassion, and will be able to explain it to you clearly, so you understand *why* you're getting this advice.

Remember: your solicitor is there to advise you what to do and it's for you to decide whether to follow that advice.

The family solicitors at Parfitt Cresswell are all experienced, compassionate, and dedicated to helping you move on to a bright future — and with that in mind we'd like to invite you to a free, face-to-face meeting (valued at £200) with one of our expert family lawyers.

You can come along to any of our offices, and be sure to find a solicitor who will understand your individual needs and who will look after your best interests.

Our family law solicitors work with many people going through a relationship breakdown and help them plan their future — at the start of a relationship as well as at the end of it. Simply call 0800 015 2843 or email us at tgdg@parfittcresswell.com and book a time to come and talk to us about your relationship.

What to Expect from Your First Meeting

Divorce and separation are life-changing events and mistakes can be expensive — so it's vital you find the right solicitor as soon as possible. Being well-prepared will help you reach the best possible outcome in the shortest time.

The Parfitt Cresswell team has worked in family law for a long time, and we know how important it is to establish what you need and how best we can help you before you make a final decision about choosing a solicitor. That's why we offer this initial meeting.

Having a good relationship with your family lawyer will make the divorce process less stressful. And that means the decision-making process will be easier — and there will be a number of decisions you'll have to make with the support of your lawyer whilst you're going through the divorce process. The initial meeting is a chance to find out whether you connect with a potential family lawyer.

You need to be sure you're willing to invest emotionally and financially to start a new stage of your life — so we make sure we offer emotional support as well as legal advice. We want you to be completely prepared for what comes next.

You'll also certainly have lots of questions at this point, especially about your home, your children, and your financial settlement. Much as we'd like to, we can't possibly give you easy answers because every divorce is different. So the more information you bring with you to our first meeting, the more we'll be able to give you an idea of what to expect.

If you can bring as much financial information as possible, as well as thinking about your goals and circumstances, that will enable us to get the most out of your first meeting. It's unlikely you'll manage to get everything together immediately, but this book has given you an idea of what you'll find helpful to bring along — and we'll be able to guide you through everything else when we meet.

First Meeting Checklist

To make the most of your first appointment you may want to bring the following along with you:

- Any correspondence you've received from your ex-spouse or their solicitor
- Any correspondence you've received from the court or other relevant third parties
- Your marriage or civil partnership certificate
- Dates and details of any previous marriages
- Your ex-spouse's name, date of birth, and address
- Your children's names and dates of birth, and the schools they attend

- Names and dates of birth of any children who are part of your family and live in the same household but are not children of you and your ex-spouse

- Details of your circumstances, such as an outline of your relationship and the issues you are experiencing

- Financial information — your and your ex-spouse's income, plus details of any assets such as bank accounts, savings, shares, other investments, pensions, trusts, cars, jewellery, antiques, estimated value of the matrimonial home and details of any mortgages, credit cards, and loans

- Details of any other property owned in the UK and overseas

- Details about what you want to achieve from the divorce settlement

- Questions you want to ask your solicitor at the first meeting

- Two forms of identification: usually your passport or driving licence along with a utility bill that's less than three months old. (This is to comply with the Anti Money Laundering Regulations)

Finally, please feel free to bring a friend along if you feel this will help support you. We don't recommend children attend unless absolutely unavoidable as we're going to be discussing some difficult issues during our meeting.

Remember — you can book your free face-to-face, no-obligation meeting anytime. Simply call 0800 015 2843 or email tgdg@parfittcresswell.com and book a time to come and talk about your relationship.

Take control of your own future today.

Notes

Jargon Explained

Divorce law made simple

Acknowledgement of Service: the form sent to the respondent — they can accept or contest the divorce

Alternative Dispute Resolution (ADR): ways of resolving disputes without going to court

Ancillary relief: an application for financial relief following the presentation of a petition for divorce, nullity or judicial separation

Annulment: a way of ending a marriage as an alternative to divorce — it's as if the marriage never took place

Arbitration: a form of ADR involving arbitration by one or more third parties

Assets: property with value and available to meet debts, commitments, or legacies, owned by a person or company

Court Bailiff: employees of Her Majesty's Courts & Tribunals Service, responsible for enforcing orders of the County Court

Barrister: a type of lawyer who works at higher levels of court, identified by the wig and gown

CAFCASS: the Children and Family Court Advisory and Support Service — a non-departmental public body in England set up to promote the welfare of children and families involved in family court

Capital: wealth in the form of money or other assets owned by a person

Capital Orders: one partner is ordered to pay a cash lump sums, transfer of property, or pension adjustment

Case Law: the law as established by the outcome of former cases

Child Arrangements Order: orders defining whom a child will live with, where, and when

Clean Break: an order which would lead to each spouse becoming financially independent of the other

Cohabitation Agreement: legal agreement reached between a couple who have chosen to live together (whether they are heterosexual or homosexual)

Collaborative Law: a legal process involving working with lawyers to end a marriage outside of the courts

Collaborative Participation Agreement: a form both partners sign when they begin the collaborative law process

Consent Order: a legally binding financial agreement between you and your ex-partner

Contract: a written or spoken agreement that is intended to be enforceable by law

Cross Petition: divorce petition issued by the respondent in response to the petitioner

Declaration of Trust: a document in which 'trustees' are appointed to hold property for 'beneficiaries'

Decree Absolute: a court's final order officially ending a marriage, enabling either party to remarry

Decree Nisi: a court order stating the date on which a marriage will end unless a good reason not to grant a divorce is produced

Decree of Judicial Separation: confirms the parties to a marriage or civil partnership are separated (but remain married / in a civil partnership)

Defending the Petition: when a respondent disagrees with the divorce petition and challenges it

Desertion: the situation where one spouse has decided not to live with the other spouse for no justifiable reason

Divorce: the termination of a marriage or marital union

Divorce Petition: paperwork sent to the respondent informing them of the impending divorce

Domestic Violence: violent or aggressive behaviour within the home, typically involving the violent abuse of a spouse or partner — but also including psychological, financial, sexual, or emotional abuse

Drafting Orders: preparing a document, filed in the court registry, which sets out the decision of the judge

Estate: all the money and property owned by a particular person

Family Arbitration: a form of private dispute resolution in which the parties enter into an agreement under which they appoint a suitably qualified person (an "arbitrator") to adjudicate a dispute and make an award. It can be used to resolve financial disputes and disputes concerning children

Financial Disclosure: gathering together the financial documents needed to come to a divorce settlement

Financial Dispute Resolution Hearing (FDR): a court appointment during which a divorcing couple can be helped towards a financial settlement

First Hearing Dispute Resolution Appointment (FHDRA): the first court hearing after an application has been made to court in private family law

Form E: your financial statement

Hearing: a proceeding before a court, usually shorter and often less formal than a trial

Income: money received, especially on a regular basis, for work or through investments

Lawyer: a person who practises or studies law, especially (in the UK) a solicitor or a barrister or (in the US) an attorney

Lodge Application: a document in which the person completing the document states his intention to seek a court order

Magistrates Courts: a lower court, where almost all criminal proceedings start and where some civil matters are also decided, notably family proceedings

Married Women's Property Act 1882: an Act of Parliament that significantly altered English law regarding the property rights of married women, which besides other matters allowed married women to own and control property in their own right

Matrimonial Causes Act 1973: an Act of Parliament governing divorce law and marriage in England and Wales

Mediation: a form of ADR, a way of resolving disputes between with a third party, the mediator, to help negotiate a settlement out of court

Mediation Information and Assessment Meeting (MIAM): a meeting to see if mediation could be used to resolve your difficulties, rather than going straight to court

Parental Responsibility: the legal rights, duties, powers, responsibilities and authority a parent has for a child and the child's property

Parental Responsibility Agreement: an agreement made between the mother and the unmarried father to allow him to have parental responsibility

Parental Responsibility Order: an order under the Children Act 1989, which unmarried fathers can apply for when the mother refuses to allow the father to be registered or re-registered on the birth certificate, or refuses to sign a Parental Responsibility Agreement with him

Pension Sharing Order: an order that a pension fund should be divided in percentages stipulated by the court

Pension Attachment Order: enables the court to direct pension scheme trustees to make payments to an ex-spouse from the date the member draws on the pension benefits

Petitioner: the spouse who petitions for divorce

Power of Arrest: a mandate that allows an individual to remove a criminal's (or suspected criminal's) liberty; can also be used to protect a person from harm or to protect from damage to property

Prenuptial Agreement: an agreement made by a couple before they marry concerning the ownership of their respective assets should the marriage fail

Process Server: delivers or "serves" legal documents to a defendant or person involved in a court case

Property Adjustment Orders: orders the court can make about the family home

Residence Order: now known as a Child Arrangements Order

Respondent: the spouse who receives the divorce petition

Round Table Negotiations: similar to the type of negotiation that would take place at court, but which take place outside court

Separation: living apart from your legal partner

Separation Agreement: also known as a Deed of Separation, it records from the start who is to have what and what both parties' responsibilities are

Solicitor: a member of the legal profession qualified to deal with legal matters

Spousal Maintenance Orders: an order for your ex-partner to pay maintenance income

Spouse: a husband or wife, considered in relation to their partner

Welfare Checklist: the checklist the court will refer to when making decisions affecting children in divorce cases

Will: a legal declaration by which someone names one or more persons to manage their estate and provides for the distribution of their property at death

About Parfitt Cresswell

I'm Teresa Payne, owner at Parfitt Cresswell. Growing up I never dreamt of being a lawyer… Until I found myself facing divorce in my late 20s. I had a seven-year-old son and the last thing I thought I'd experience was my relationship ending and having to start again.

To be honest, I didn't know where to turn. The road ahead felt like an enormous mountain and I didn't have the emotional or physical strength to even take the first step of the climb. Fortunately, I had a good friend who supported me through this. With her encouragement, I went along to my local solicitors feeling confident they'd be able to help me.

They were qualified professionals and advertised "family law" so I thought I was in good hands. I think most would agree that was a reasonable assumption — but after experiencing their non-existent client care and paying substantial legal fees for a very poor service and very little practical advice, I decided I could do far better than this myself.

I started researching "how to divorce", "what happens to the family home when couples separate", and "where will the children live after divorce" — all those questions that wake you up in the night when it feels like your world is falling apart.

My Mission In Life

My research was daunting and time-consuming but it sparked an interest to learn more about our legal system. This interest, and my desire to help others going through separation and divorce, changed my direction in life. I decided to use the funds I received from my divorce to train as a solicitor — and spent the next seven years studying until I qualified in 2004.

At the start of my professional life I worked face-to-face, individually, with many clients helping them through some of the most difficult times in their lives. It was so rewarding to help others navigate the legal and emotional maze and help them find their new life so that they could start again.

As my client numbers grew I realised I needed more 'me's if I was going to fulfil my mission of helping as many people as possible navigate the divorce process. So in 2007 I bought my own law firm, Parfitt Cresswell. We started in a small office in Fulham Broadway in West London.

Over the past ten years, I've focused on growing a specialist family law team of qualified lawyers who share the same values as I do. They work hard to provide the very best standards of client support and legal advice to all our family law clients. They're all experts in family law and are all Members of Resolution, which means they're committed to taking a conciliatory approach to helping you achieve the best settlement results possible in your situation. However, if it becomes clear your ex or their legal advisor isn't adopting a conciliatory approach, my family lawyers are more than willing to play hard ball if necessary.

My team also understands the emotional pressures you're going through and will support you and, in some cases, introduce you to other professionals who can help — like therapists and counsellors.

This Isn't About Revenge

My mission is very clear — I want to help you get the best possible outcome for you and your family. So if you're feeling angry and looking for revenge, and you want to hurt your ex as much as possible, we're not the law firm for you.

I completely understand why you may be feeling so angry at the thought of your relationship ending, but revenge isn't going to help you move on in your life. We would not be helping you by accepting your instructions and we would not be honouring our commitment and mission to help people through their relationship breakdown and reach their best settlement.

There are plenty of law firms who will accept your instructions and take your money... and you may even find this eases your anger for a while. But in the long run it all too often leads to even more stress and heartache for you. I've never seen revenge bring anyone any peace.

It's really important to remember that ending a relationship is a huge event and fear of the unknown can be paralysing — even when you *know* the relationship has broken down. My advice is this: understand your emotional position but try to take a balanced and objective view about how you are going to reach a settlement that works for you and your ex.

We're here to help people who are looking for expert help navigating through the divorce process. People who want to achieve the best settlement they can in their circumstances — and keep a civilised relationship with their ex if they need to, which is particularly important if you have children. Because of this, we ask all our clients to meet us in person for a free consultation. This gives you the opportunity to tell us about your situation and your goals, and it gives us the opportunity to show you what we offer. We only accept clients we believe we can work with and truly help.

Give us a call on: 0800 015 2843.

Or email: tgdg@parfittcresswell.com

And book your meeting today.

Whichever route you choose I, and my co-author Vanessa, wish you well in your search for happiness in your new life.

Teresa J. Payne
Parfitt Cresswell